Preface

The primary goal of this book is to provide CAD practice exercises for beginners. This book contains 100 2D CAD exercises and 50 3D CAD exercises. Each exercise can be designed on any CAD software such as AutoCAD, SolidWorks, Catia, PTC Creo Parametric, Siemens NX, Autodesk Inventor, Solid Edge, DraftSight and other CAD programs. These exercises are designed to help you test out your basic CAD skills. Each exercise can be assigned separately. No exercise is a prerequisite for another. All dimensions are in mm.

✓ Click to download original 150 AutoCAD (DWG) files.

Disclaimer

The book contains 100 2D and 50 3D exercises to enable you practice what you learn. The exercises range from easy to expert level. These exercises are not tutorials. It is a practice book. You can use these exercises to improve your skills in any CAD software.

No part of this publication may be reproduced, stored in a retrieval system or transmitted in any form or
By any means electronic, mechanical, photocopying, recording or sold in whole or in part in any form, otherwise without the prior written Permission of the author or CADin360.com
All trademarks and registered trademarks appearing in this guide are the property of their respective owners.

  ✓ **Click to download original 150 AutoCAD (DWG) files.**

Acknowledgments

This book would not have been possible without a great deal of support. First, I would like to thank my parents for allowing me to realize my own potential. All the support they have provided me over the years was the greatest gift anyone has ever given me. Also, I need to thank Hira Nand Jha, who taught me the value of hard work and an education. Without him, I may never have gotten to where I am today. Next, I need to thank all the people who create such a good atmosphere.

2D EXERCISES

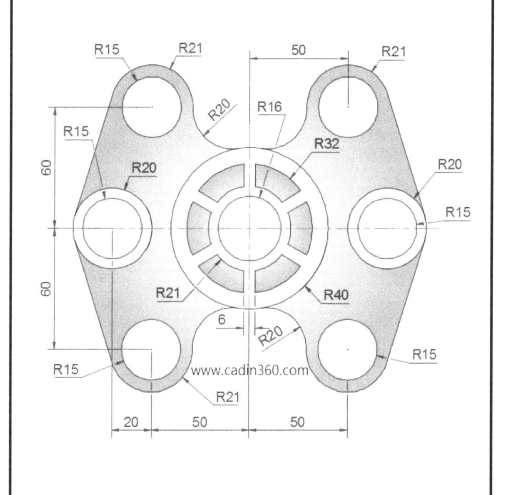

R15   R21   50   R21
R20   R16
R15   R32
R20   R20
60   R15
60
R21   R40
6
R20
R15   www.cadin360.com
R21
20   50   50   R15

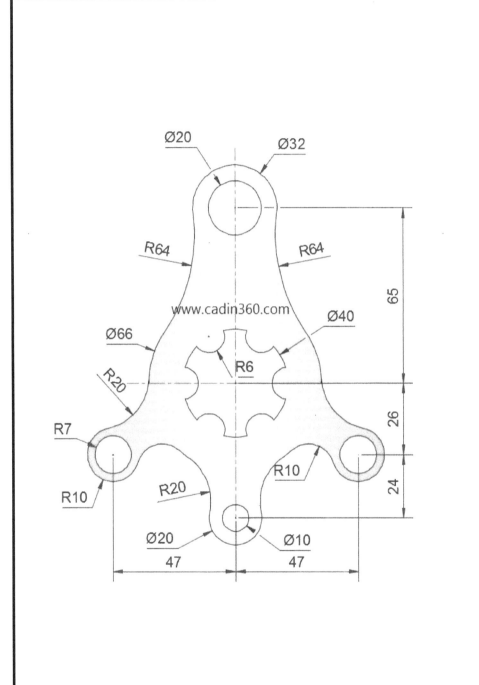

Ø20   Ø32

R64   R64

65

www.cadin360.com

Ø66   Ø40

R6

R20

26

R7

R10

R10

R20

24

Ø20   Ø10

47   47

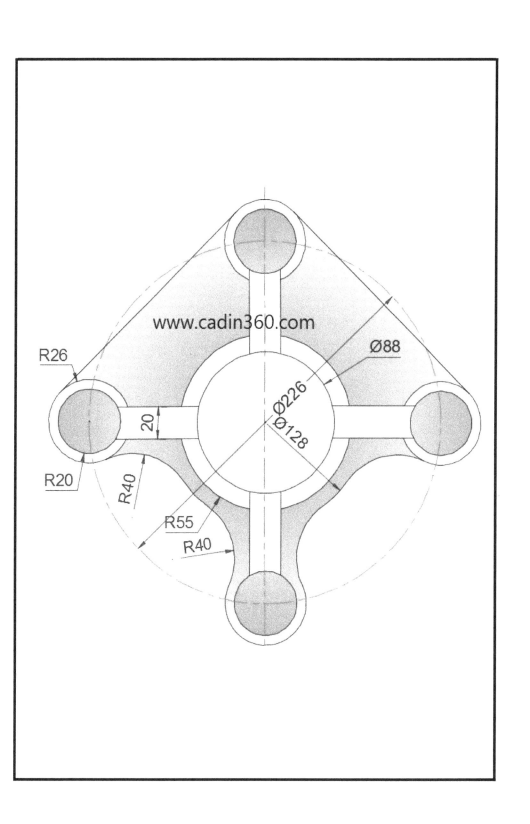
www.cadin360.com

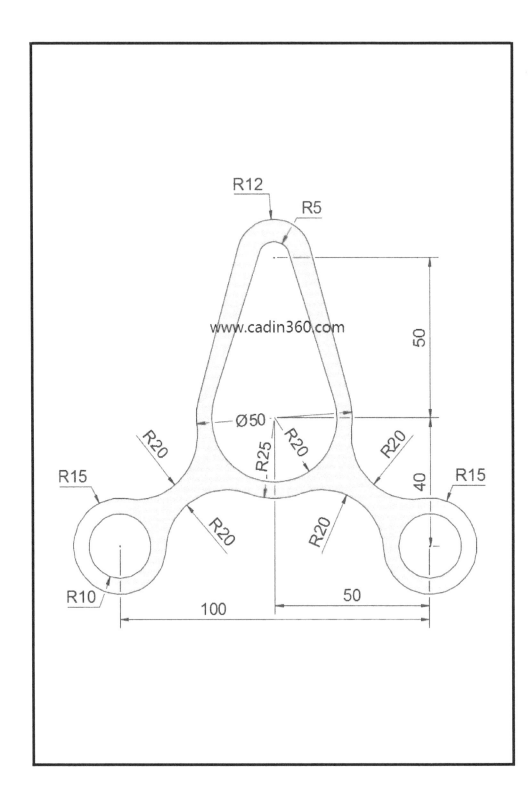

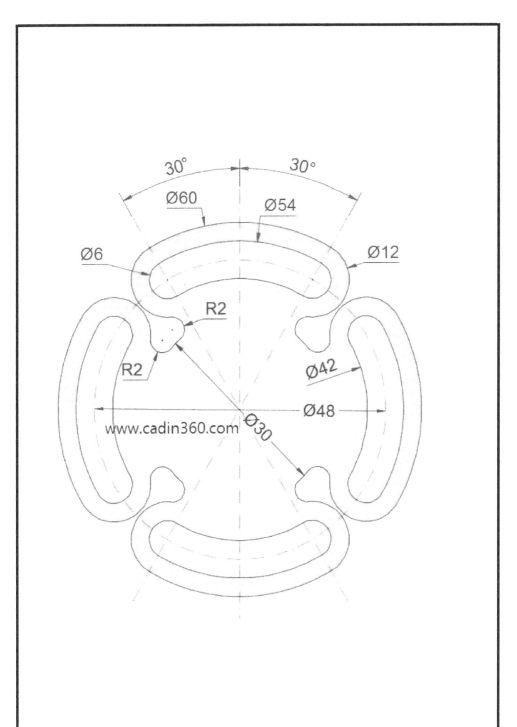

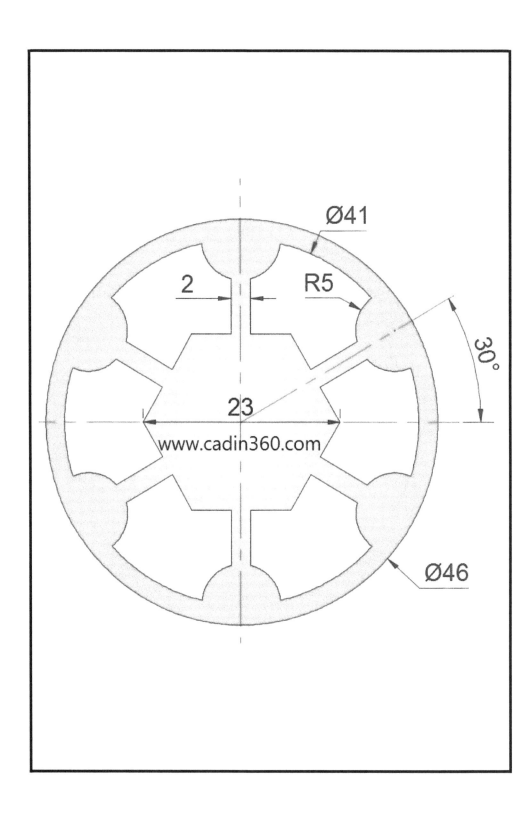

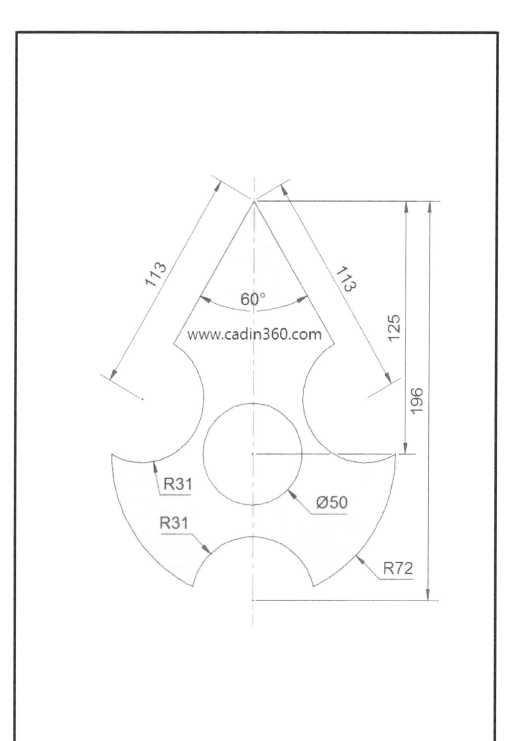

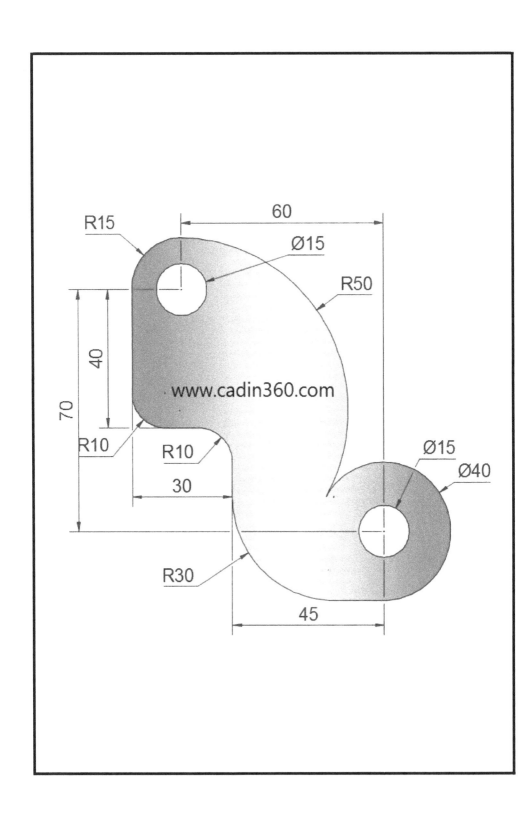

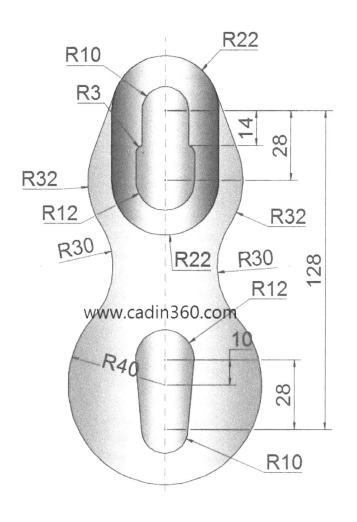

R10 R22
R3
14
28
R32
R12
R32
R30 R22 R30
R12
www.cadin360.com
10
R40
128
28
R10

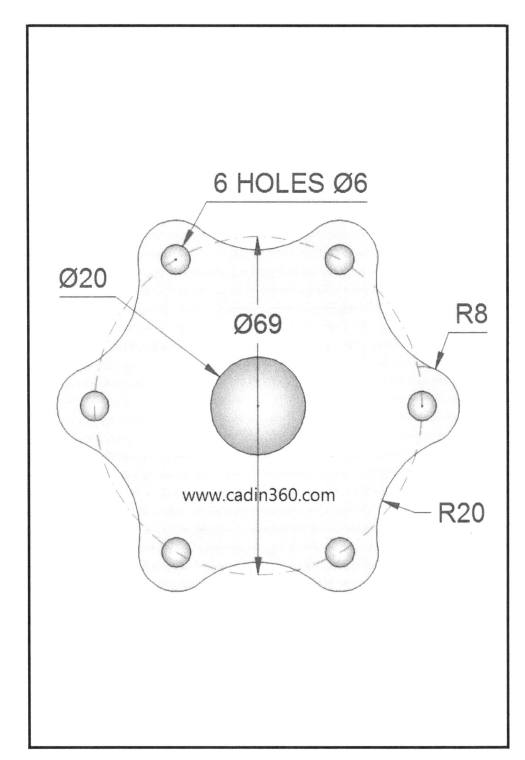

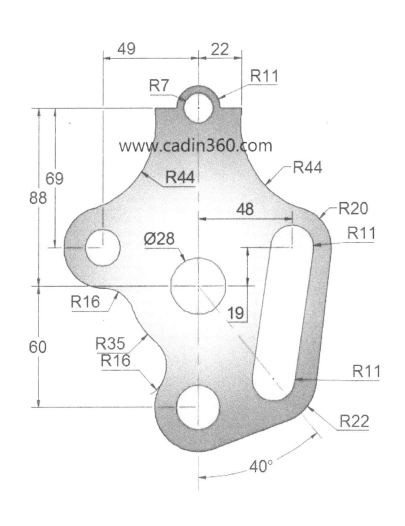

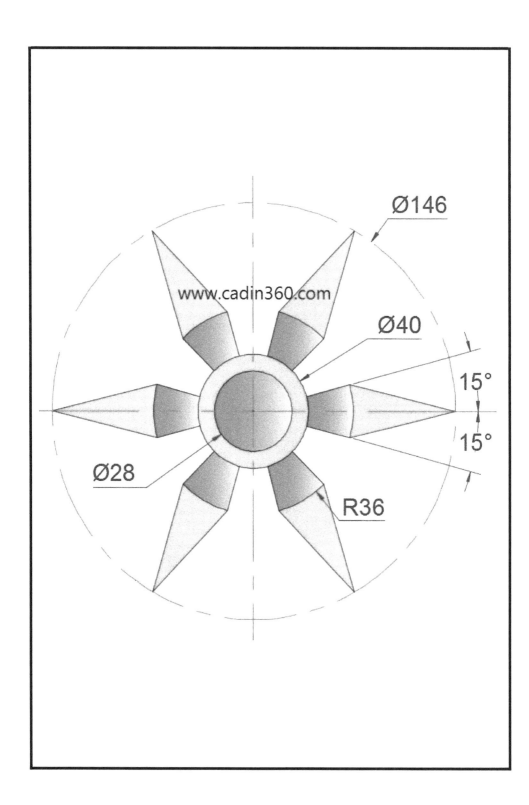

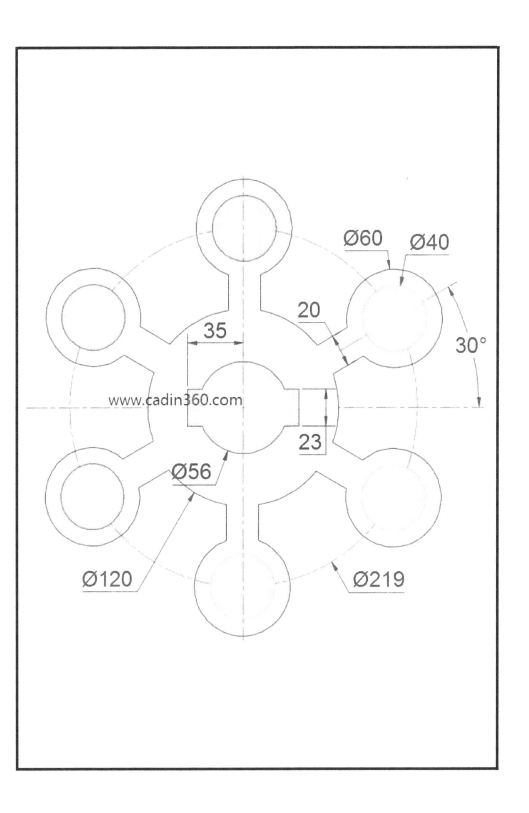

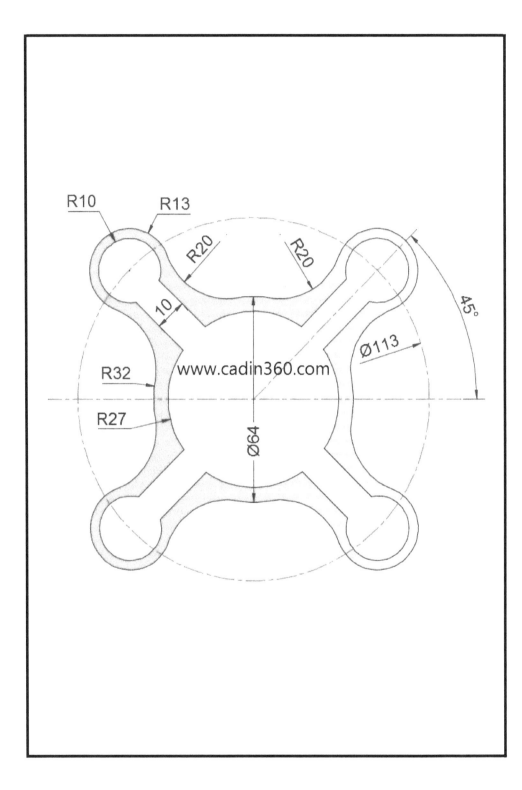

R10 R13

R20 R20

R10

R32

R27

www.cadin360.com

Ø113

45°

Ø64

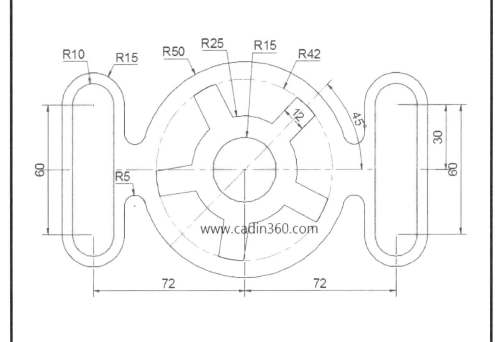

R10　R15　R50　R25　R15　R42

12

45°

60　30　60

R5

www.cadin360.com

72　72

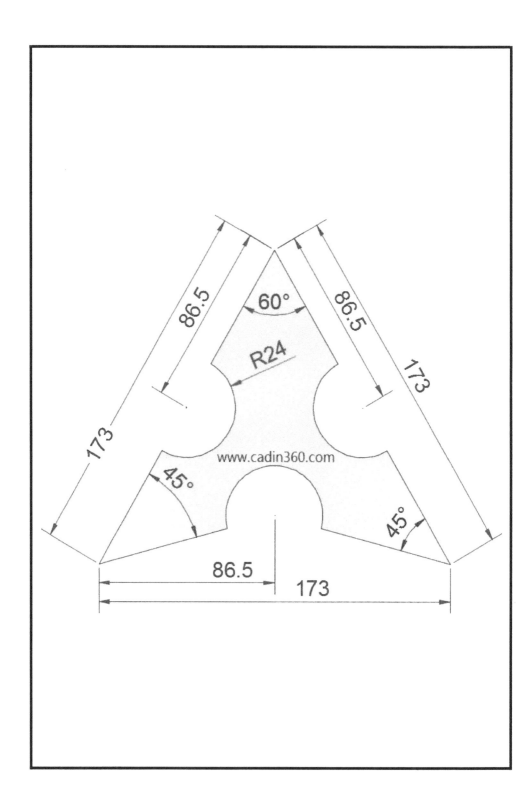

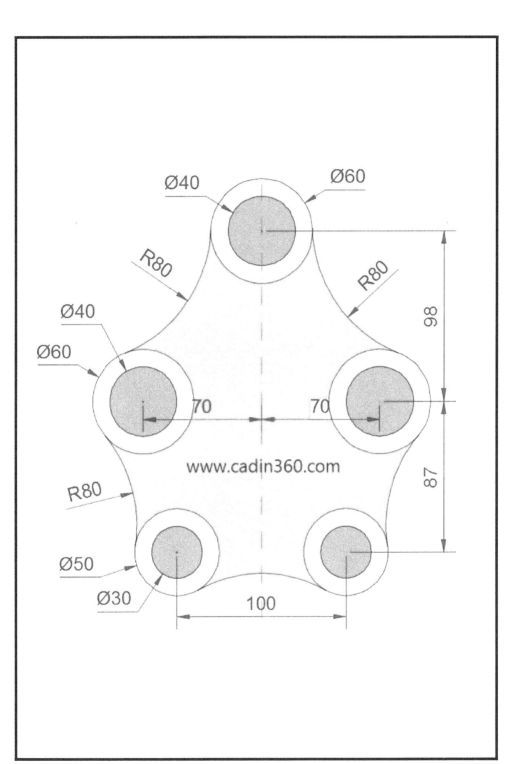

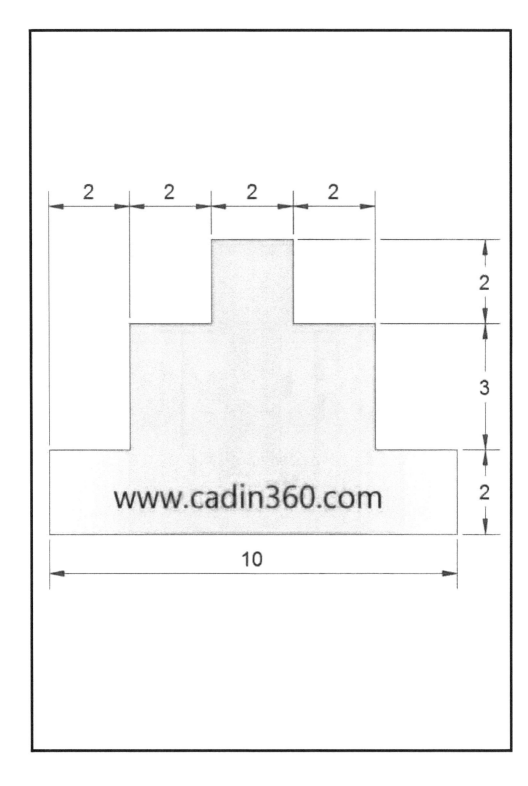

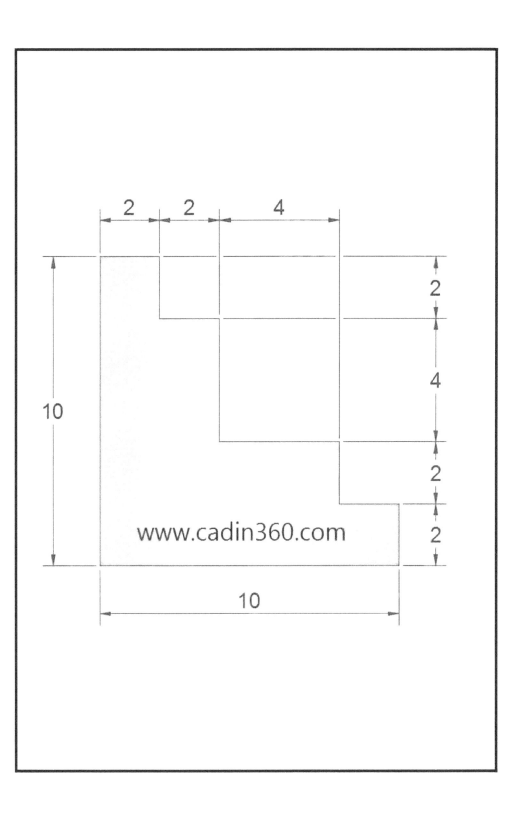

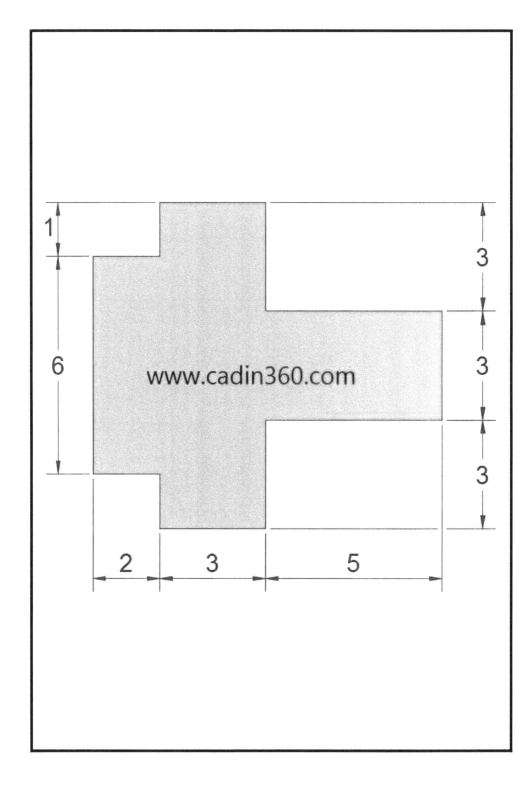

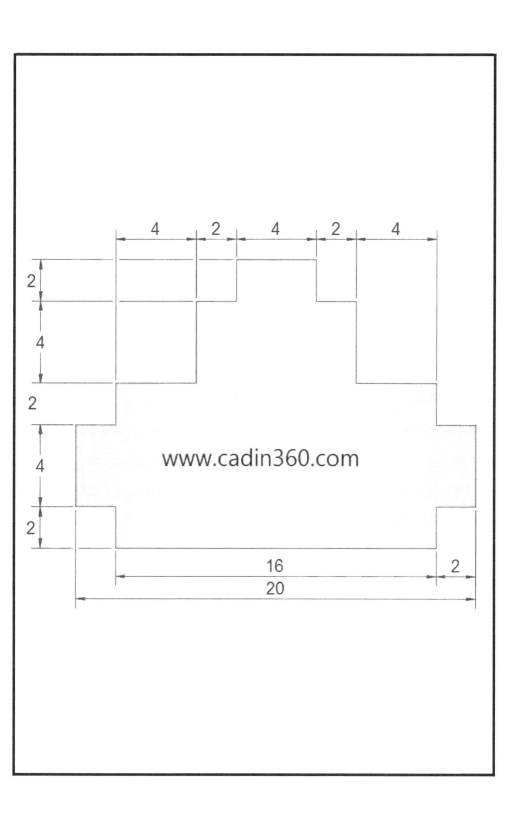

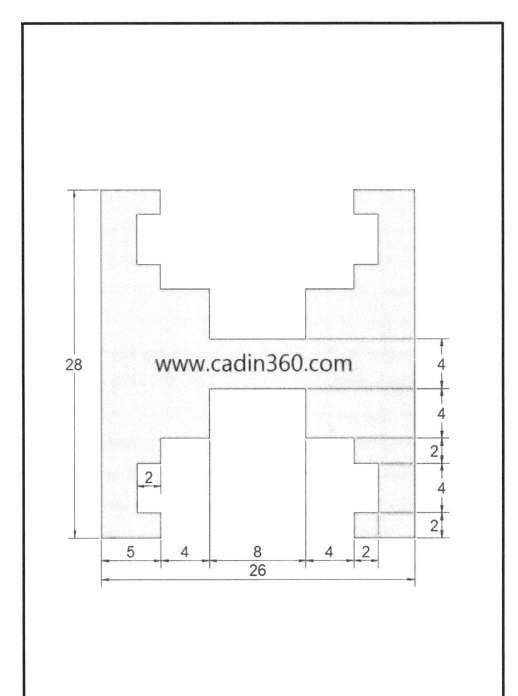

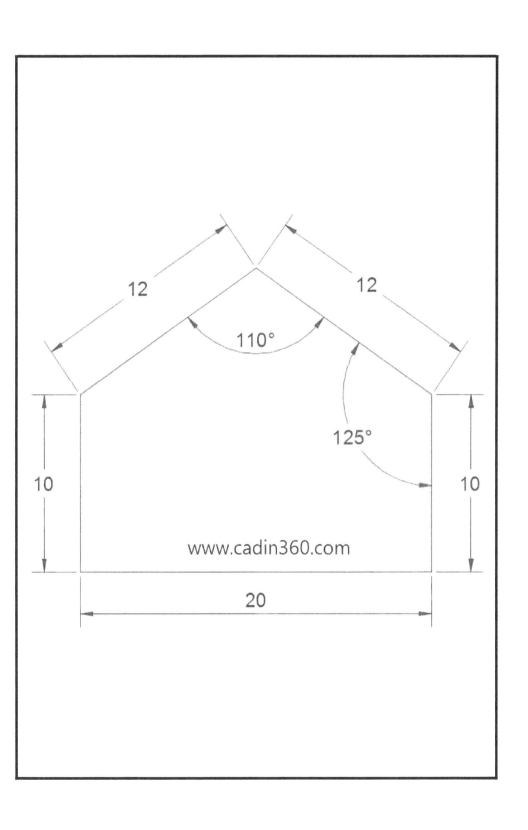

12

12

110°

125°

10

10

www.cadin360.com

20

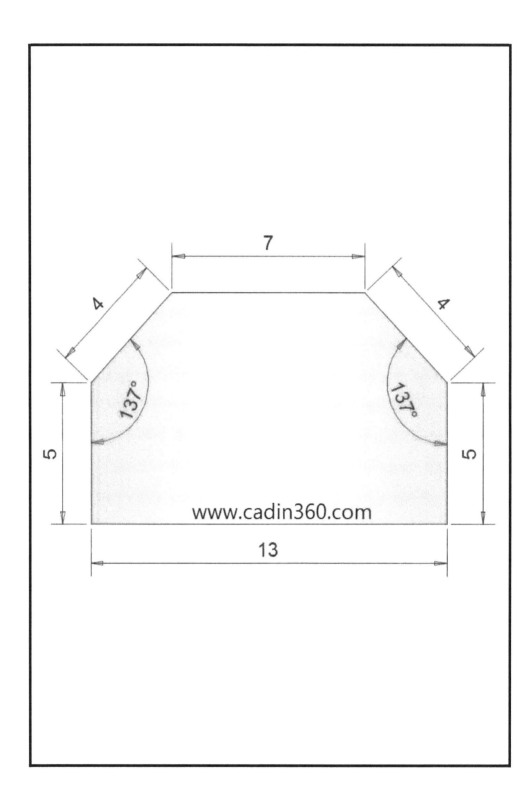

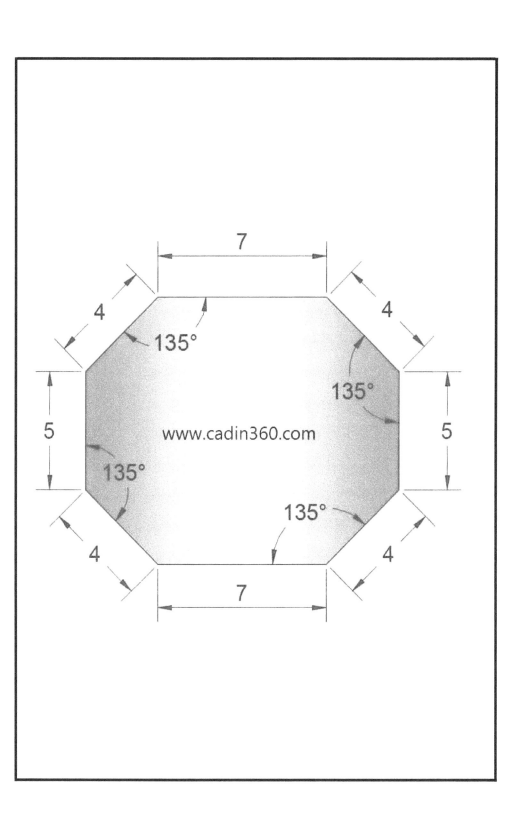

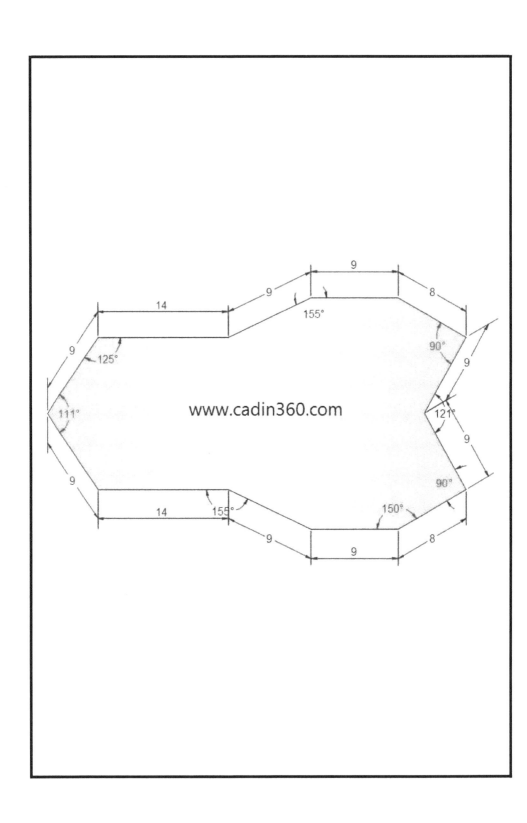
www.cadin360.com

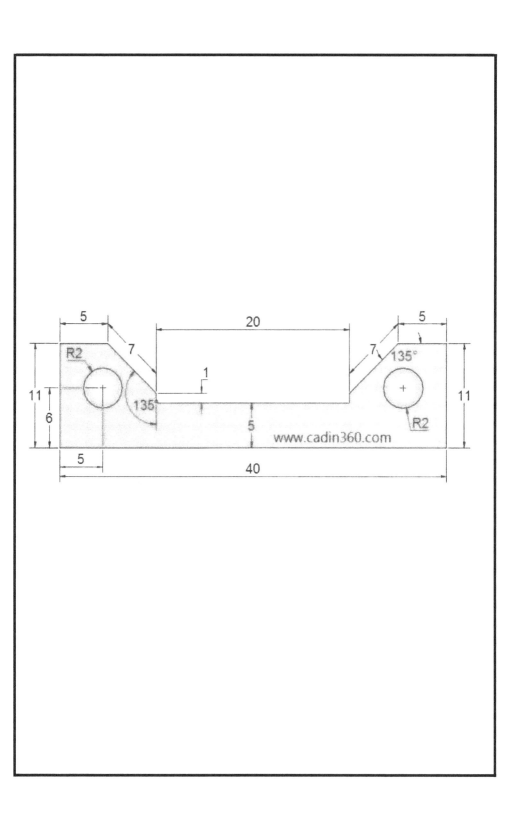

www.cadin360.com

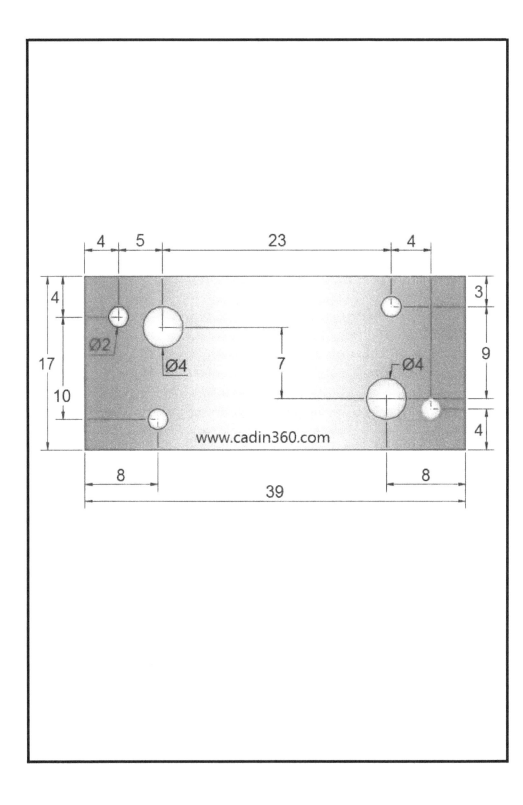

www.cadin360.com

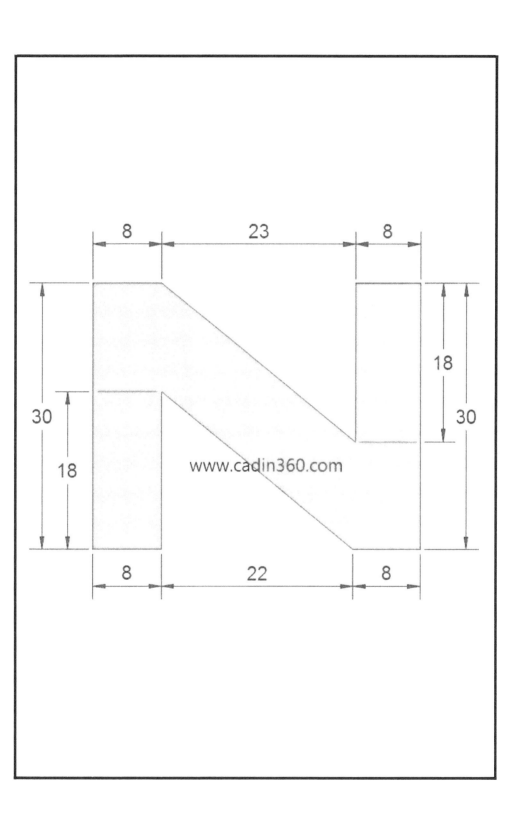

www.cadin360.com

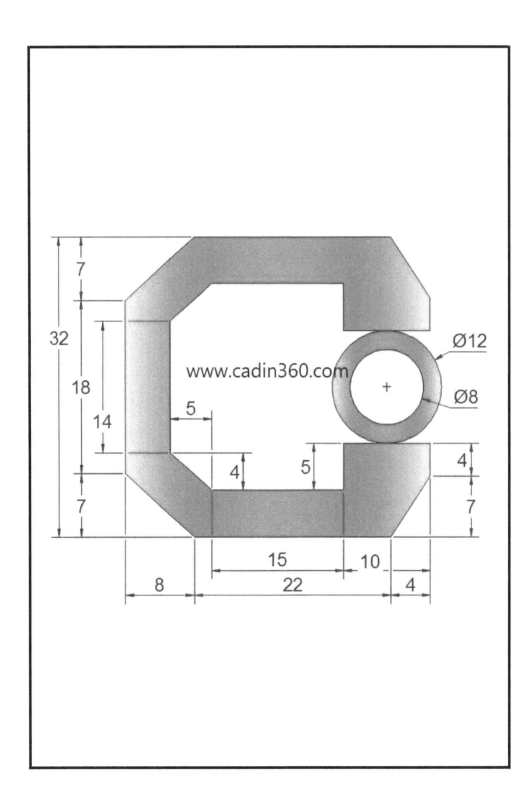

www.cadin360.com

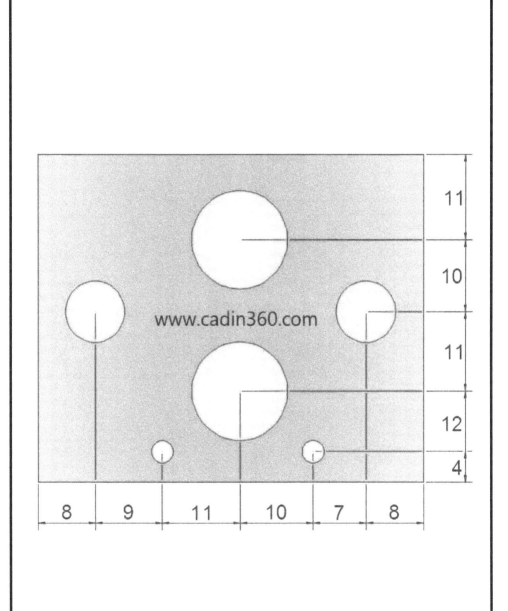

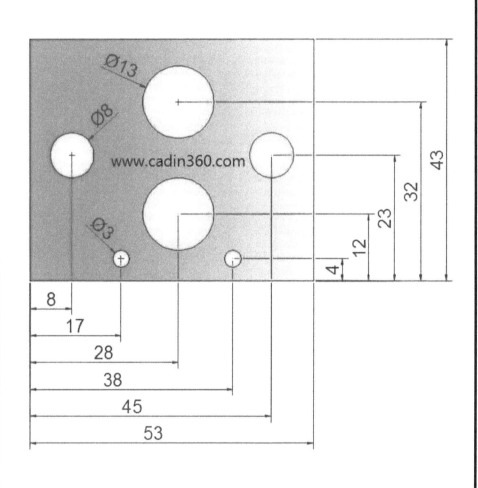

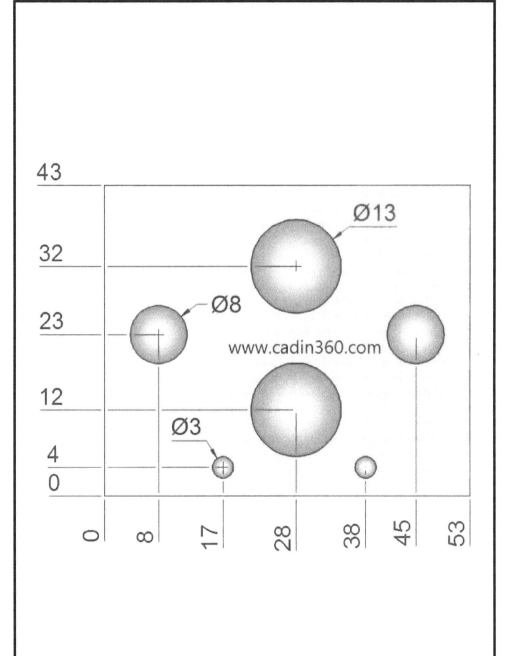

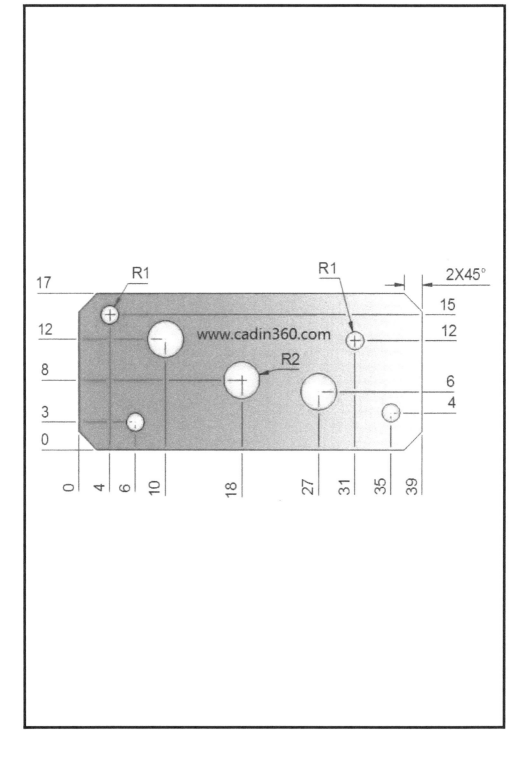

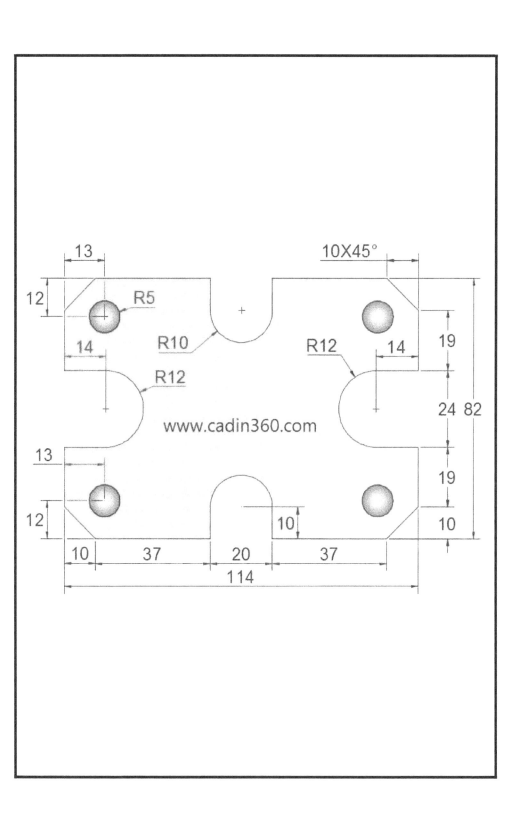

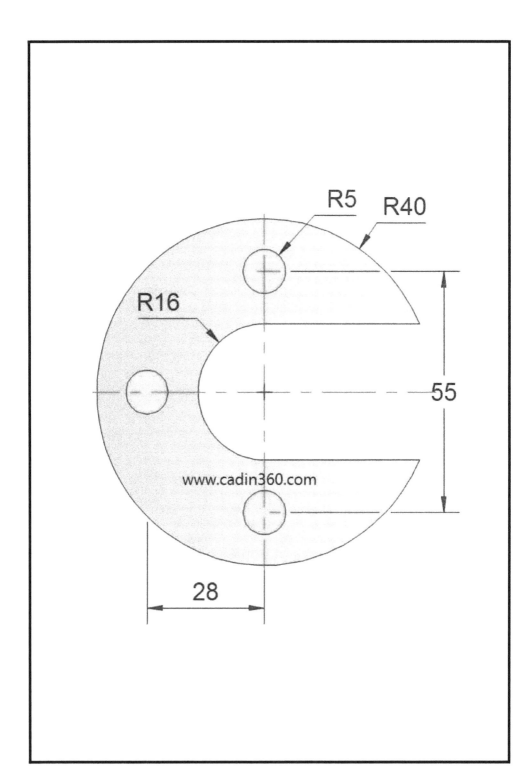

R5 R40

R16

55

28

www.cadin360.com

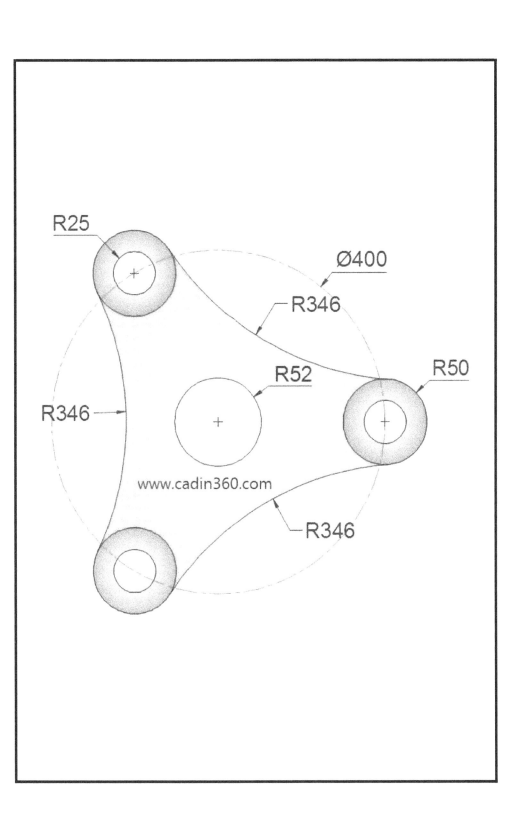

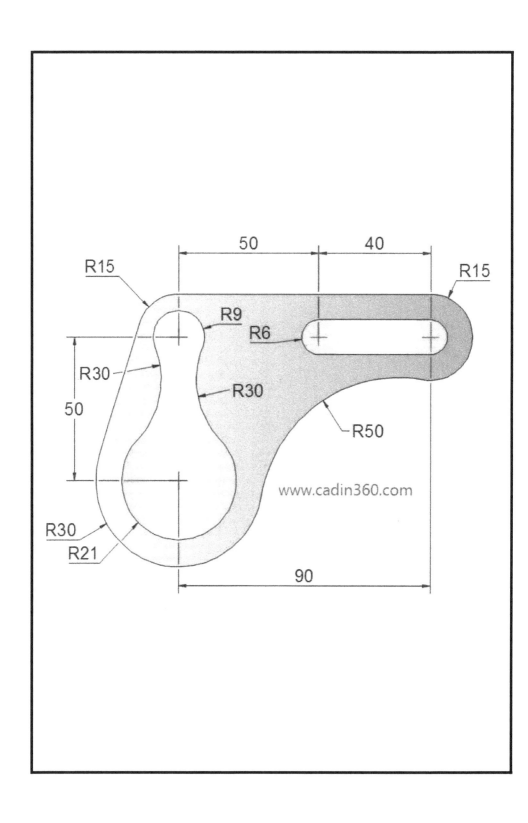

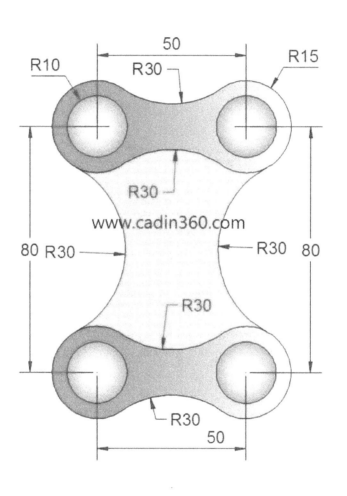

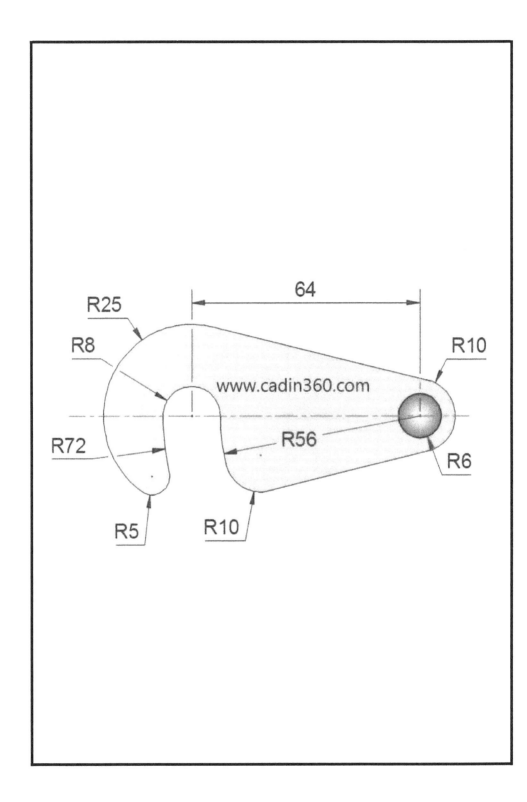

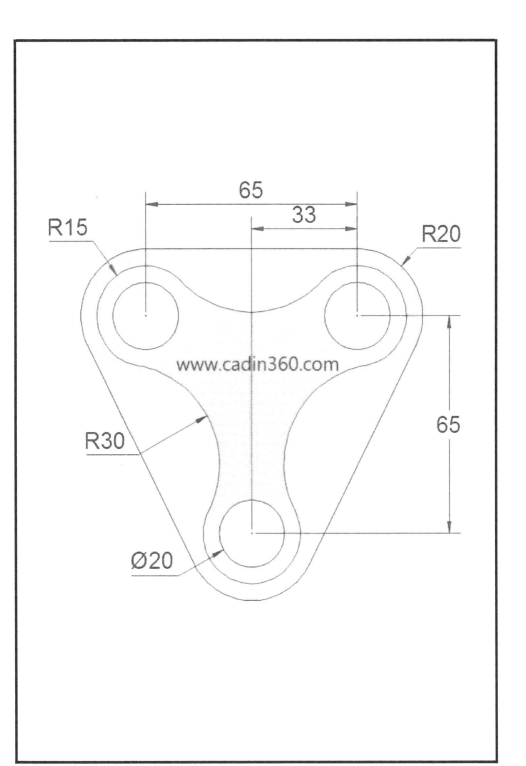

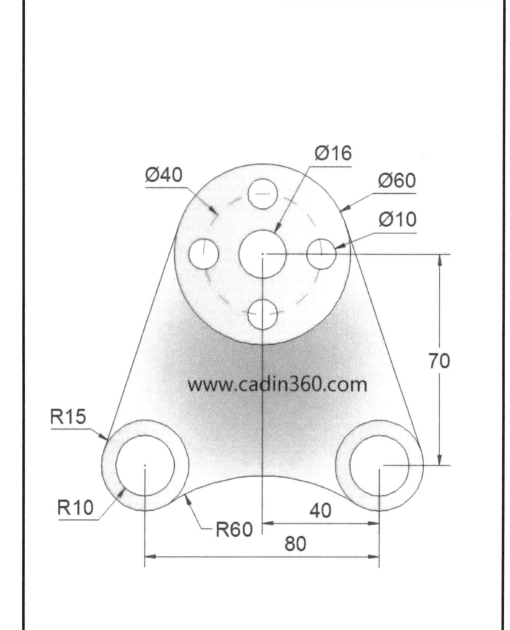

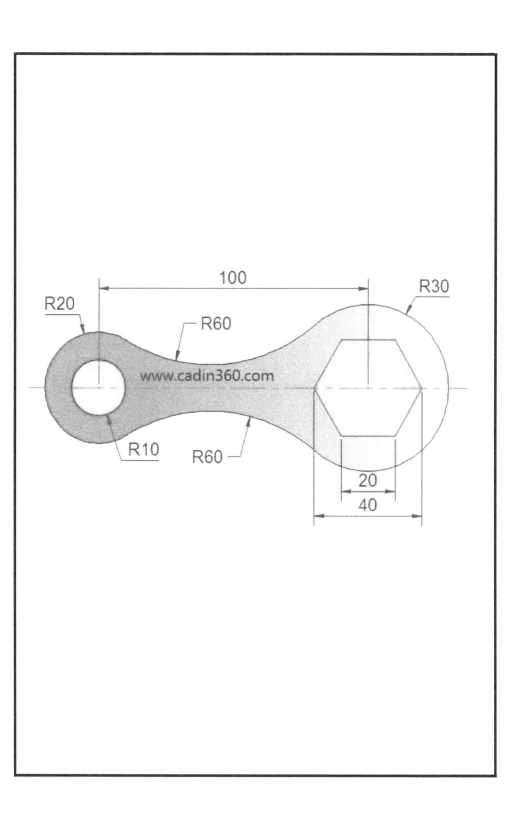

R20
R60
R10
R60
100
R30
www.cadin360.com
20
40

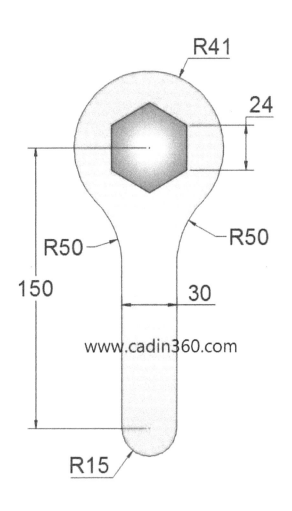

R41

24

R50

R50

150

30

www.cadin360.com

R15

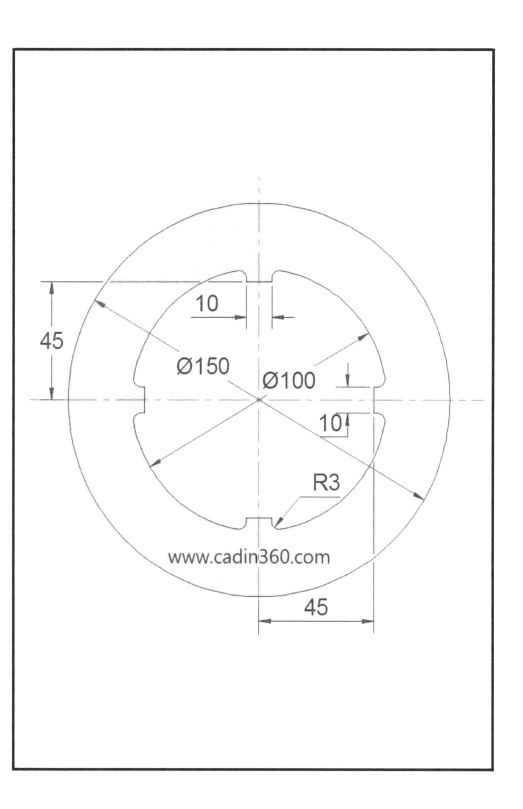

10

45

Ø150

Ø100

10

R3

www.cadin360.com

45

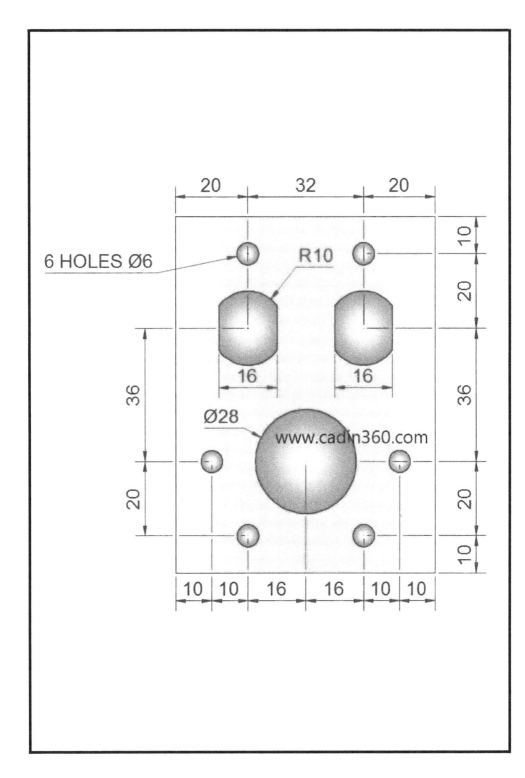

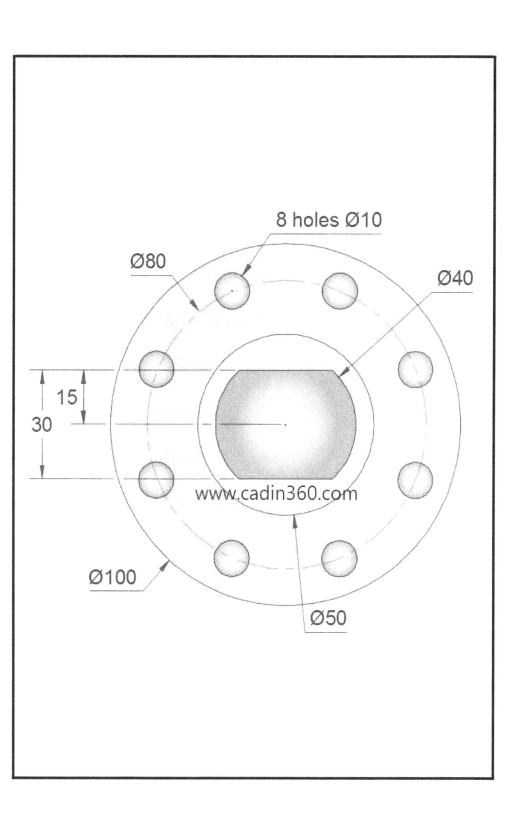

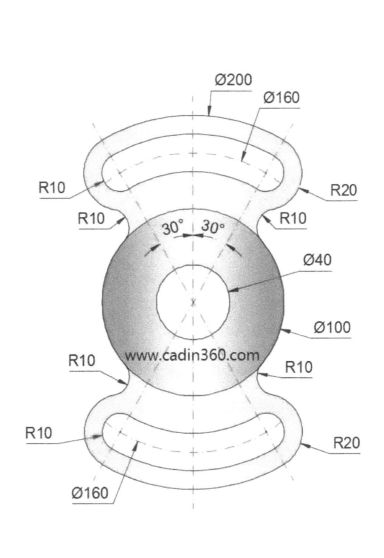

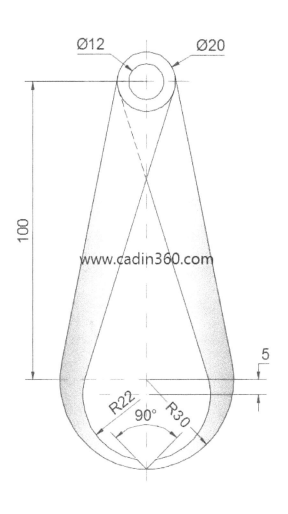

Ø12 Ø20

100

5

R22 90° R30

www.cadin360.com

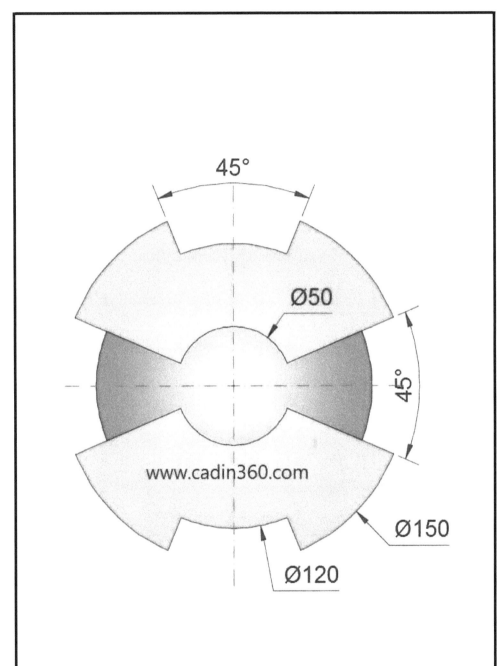

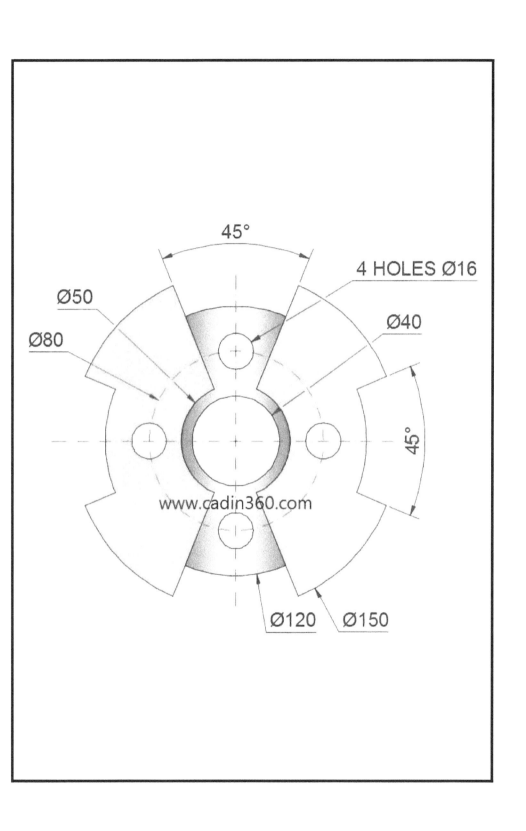

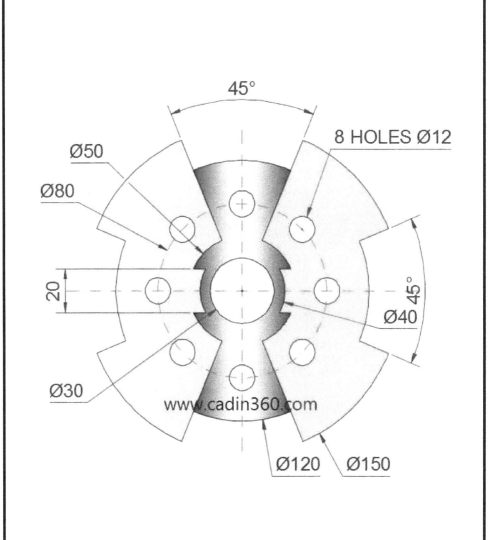

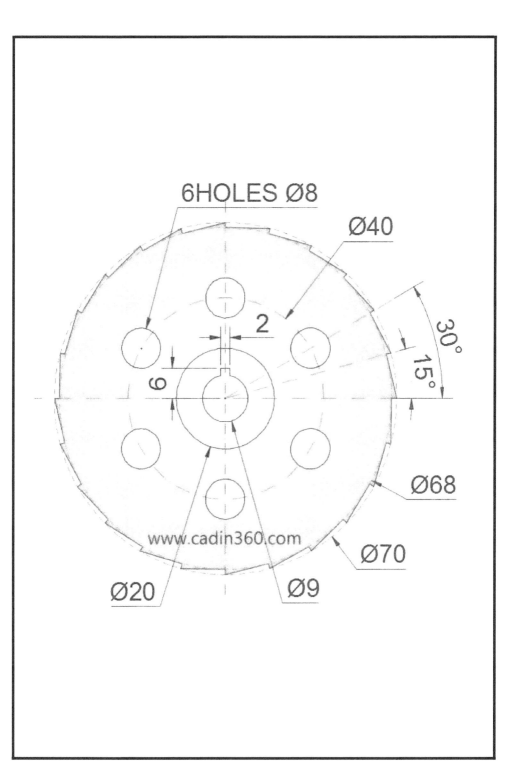

6HOLES Ø8

Ø40

30°

15°

2

9

Ø68

Ø70

Ø20

Ø9

www.cadin360.com

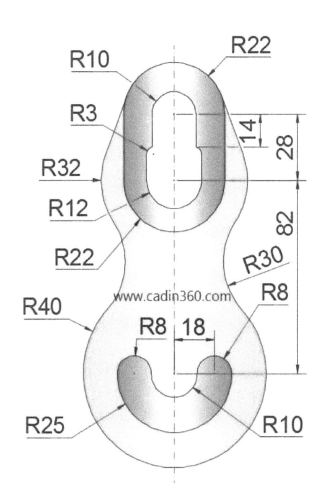

R10 R22

R3

R32

R12

R22

R40

R25

R30

R8

R8 18

R10

14

28

82

www.cadin360.com

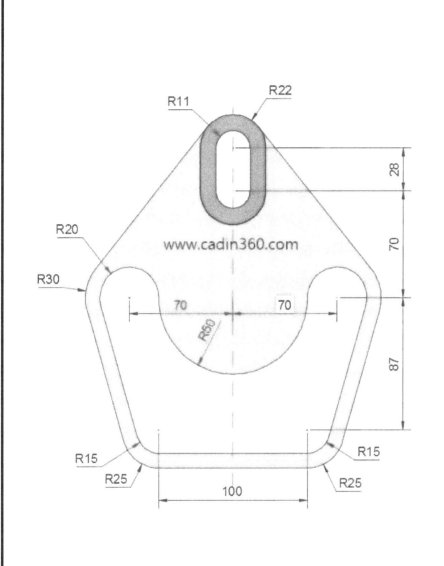

R11　R22

R20

R30

www.cadin360.com

R50

70　70

28

70

87

R15

R15

R25

R25

100

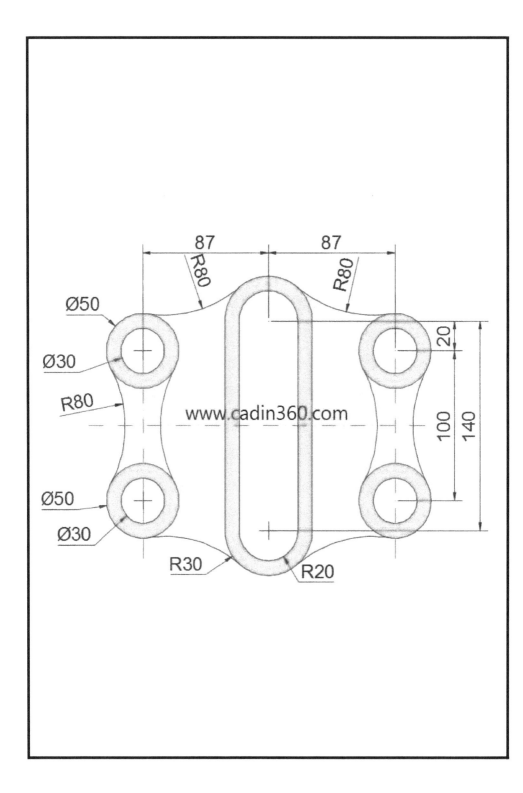

87 87

R80 R80

Ø50

Ø30

R80

www.cadin360.com

20

100 140

Ø50

Ø30

R30 R20

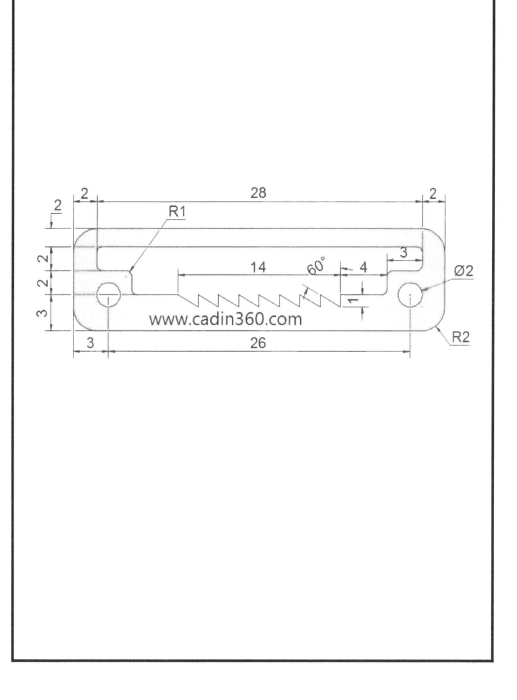

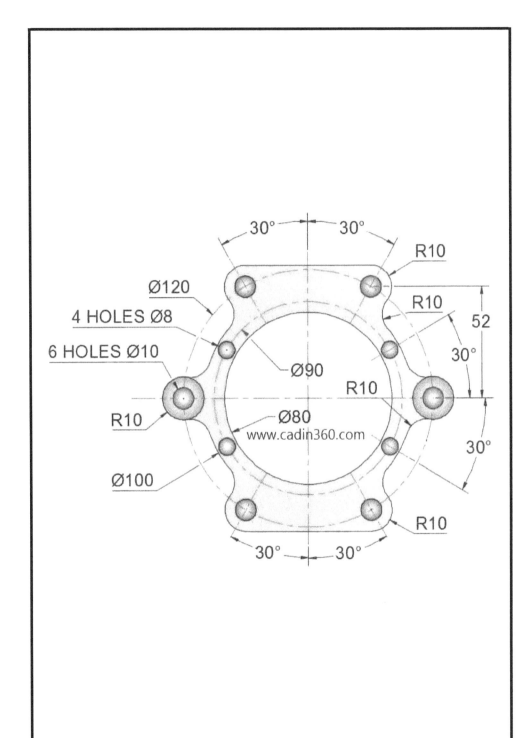

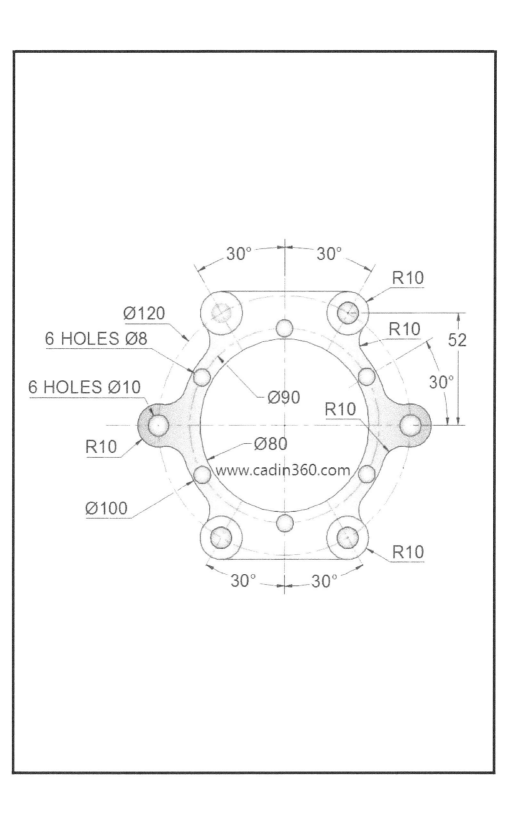

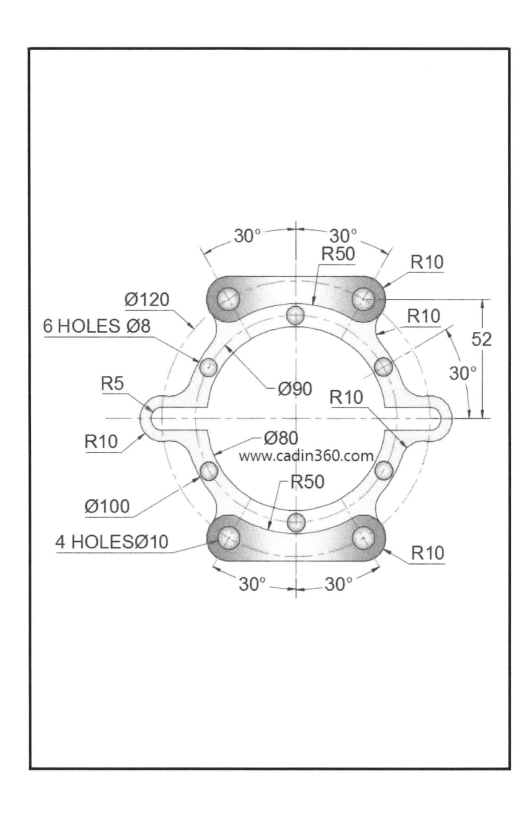

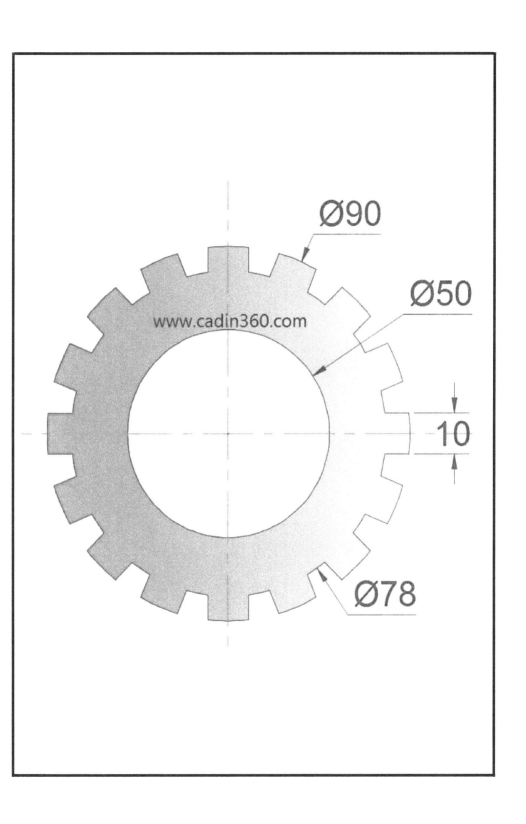

Ø90

Ø50

10

Ø78

www.cadin360.com

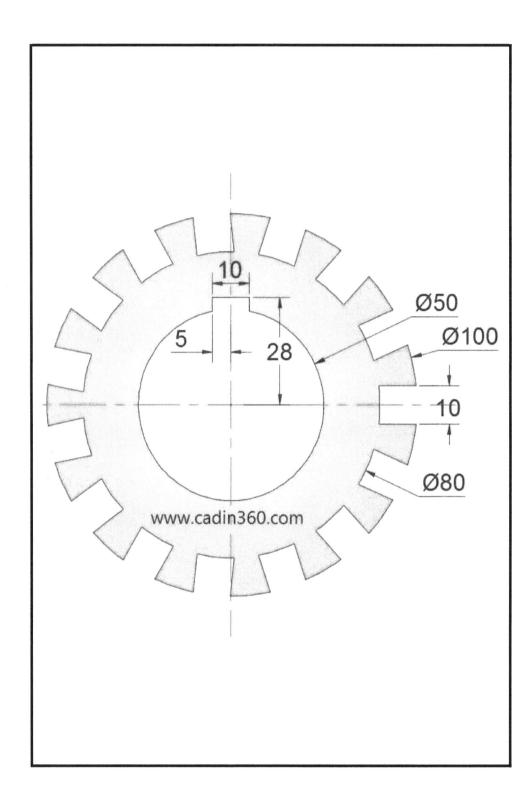

www.cadin360.com

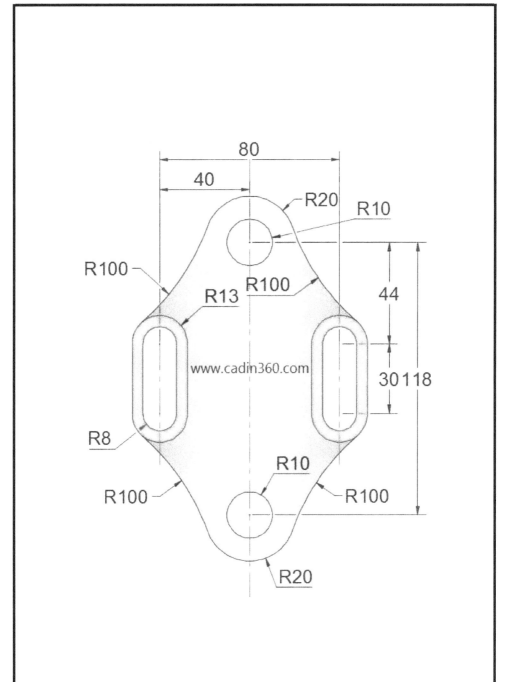

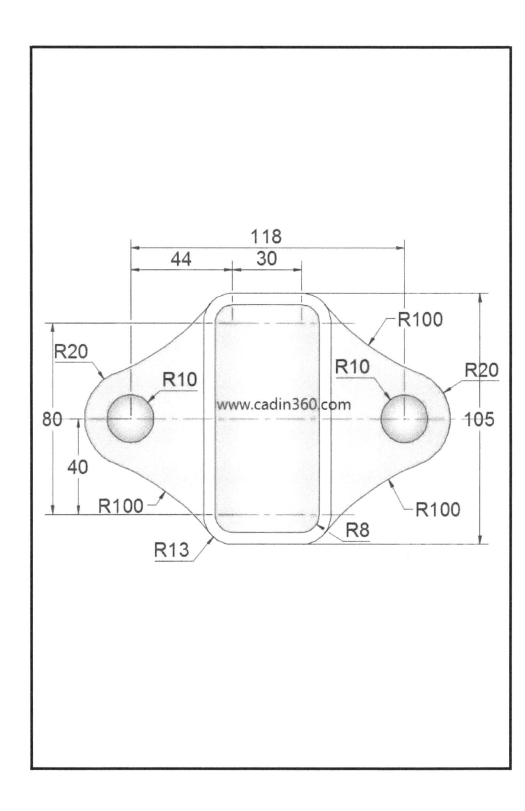

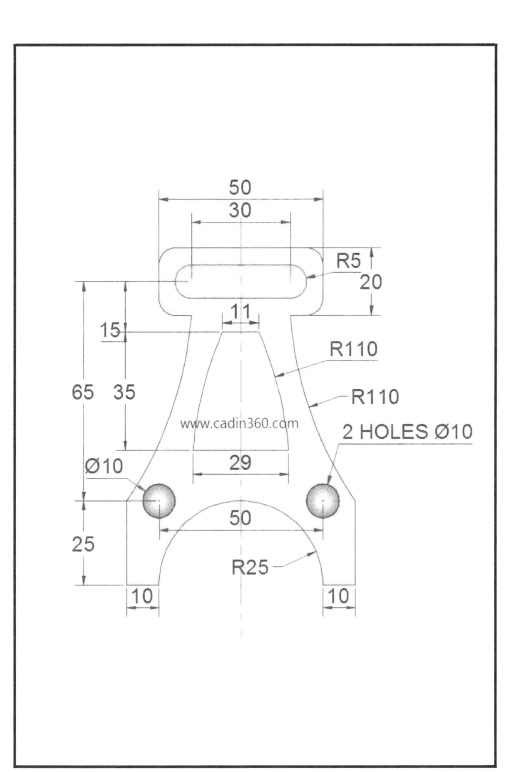

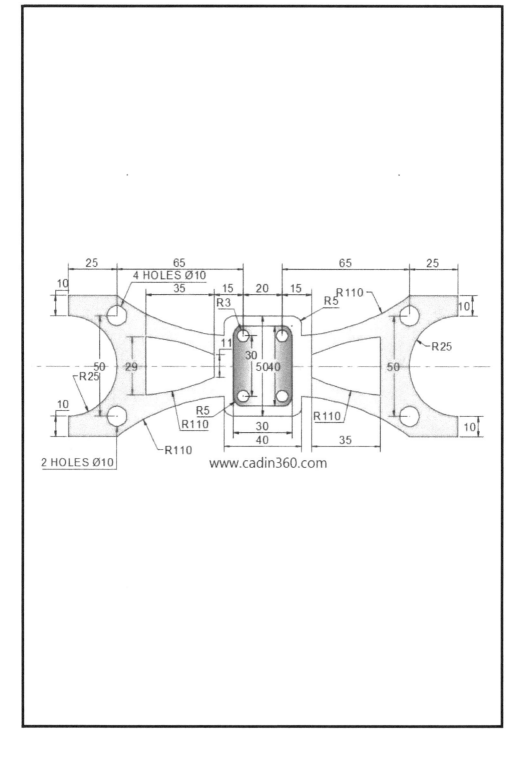

www.cadin360.com

www.cadin360.com

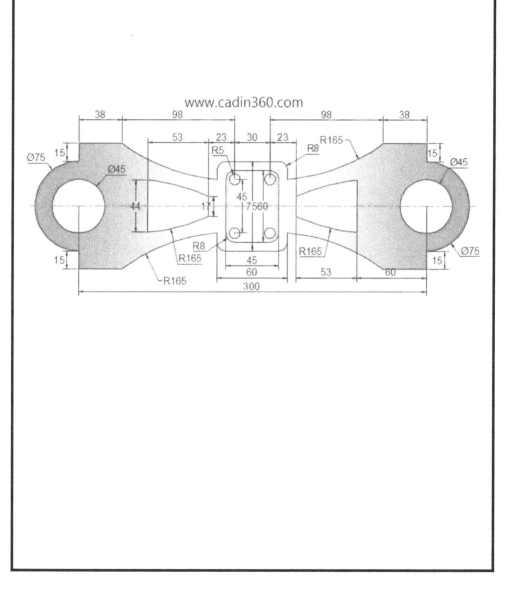

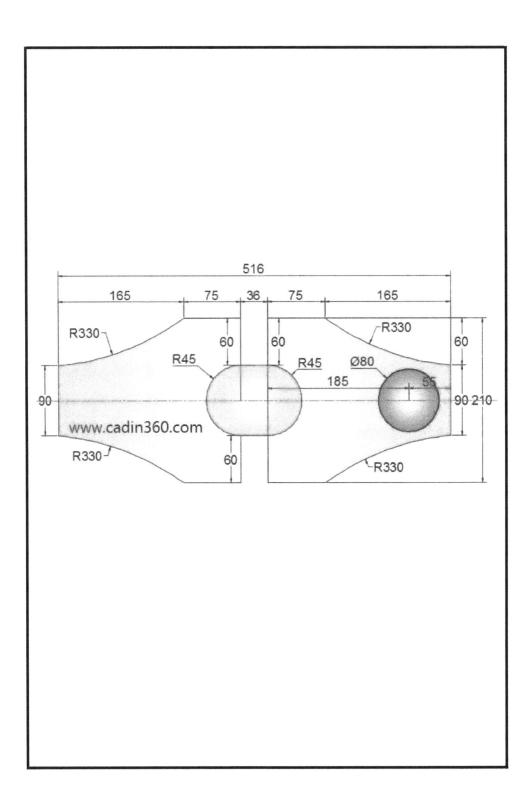

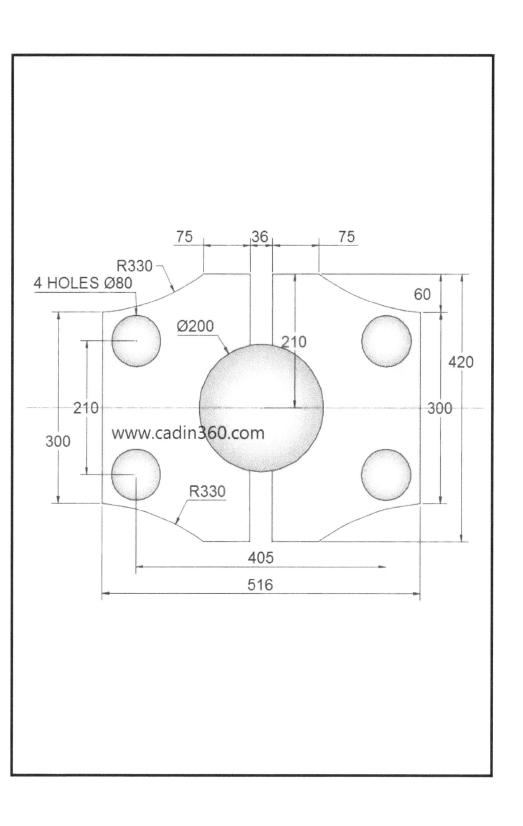

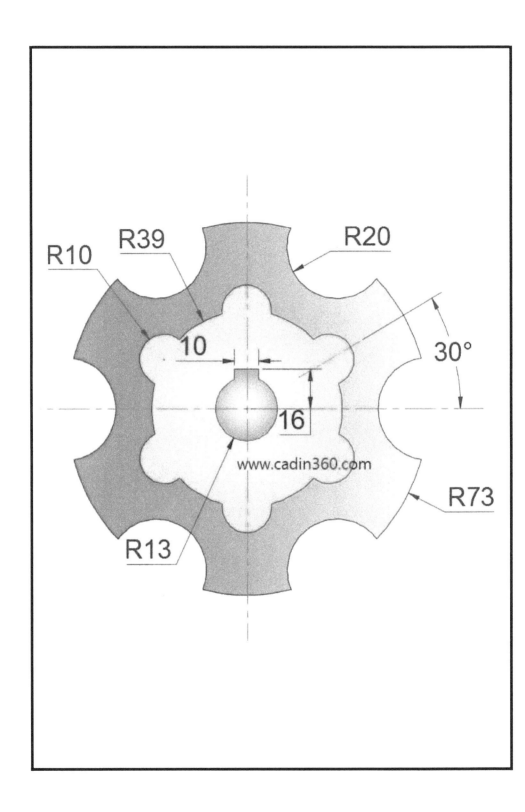

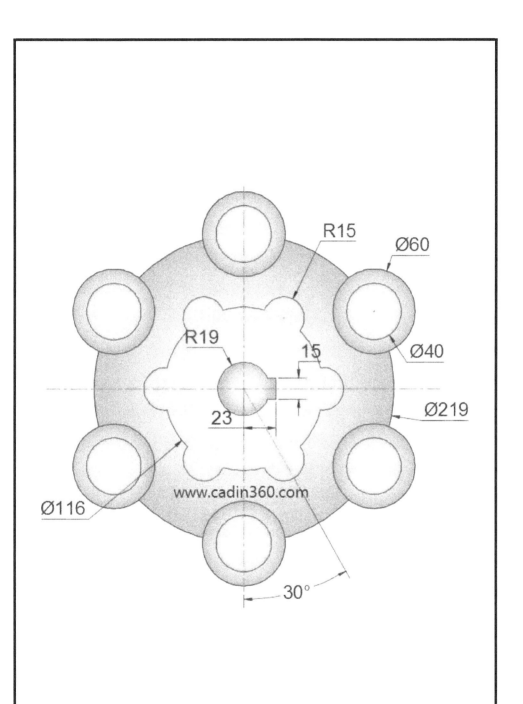

R15

Ø60

R19

15

Ø40

Ø219

23

www.cadin360.com

Ø116

30°

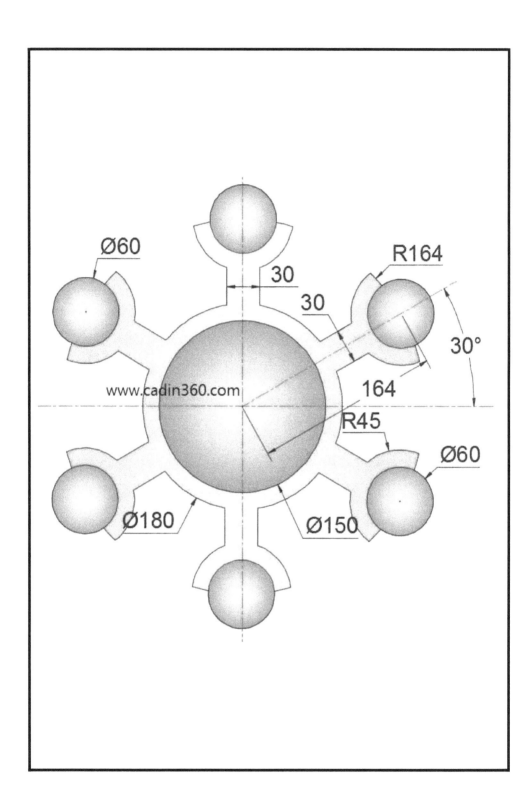

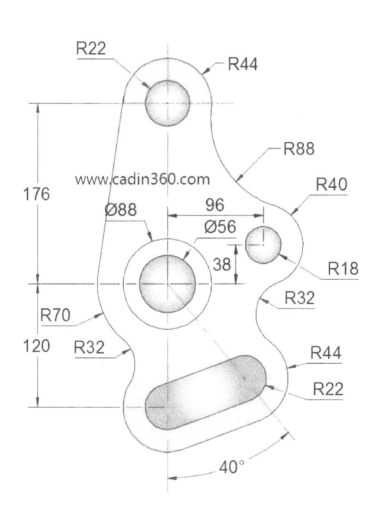

R22 R44

R88

R40

176 www.cadin360.com

Ø88 96 R18

Ø56 R32

38

R70

120 R32 R44

R22

40°

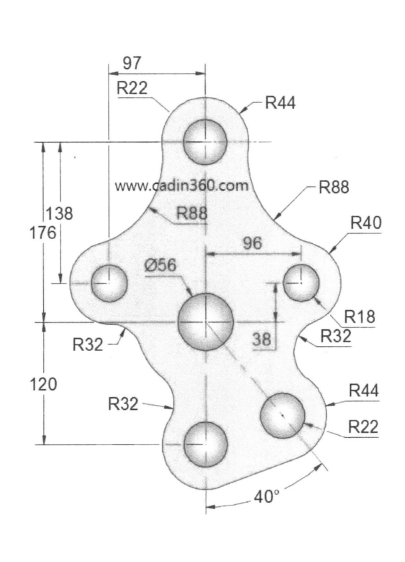

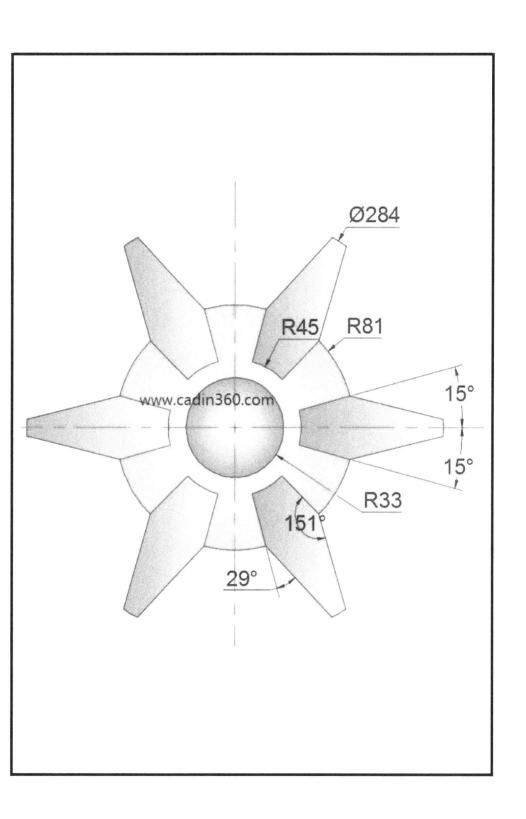

Ø284

R45 R81

15°

15°

R33

www.cadin360.com

151°

29°

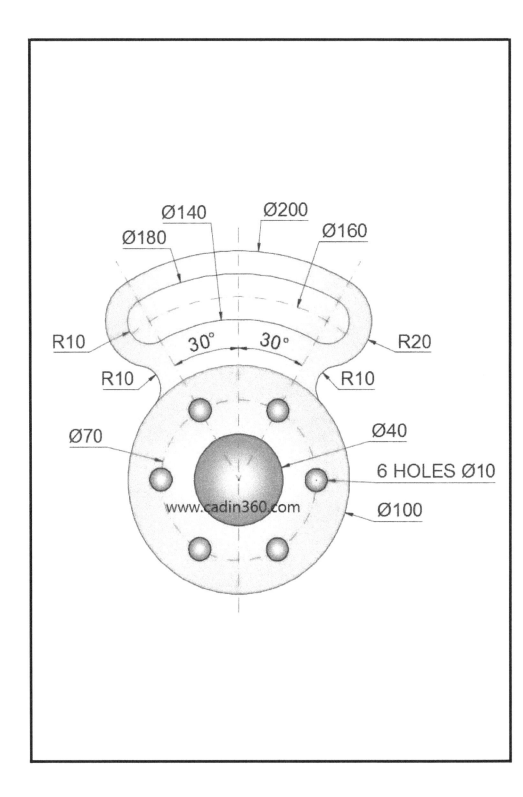

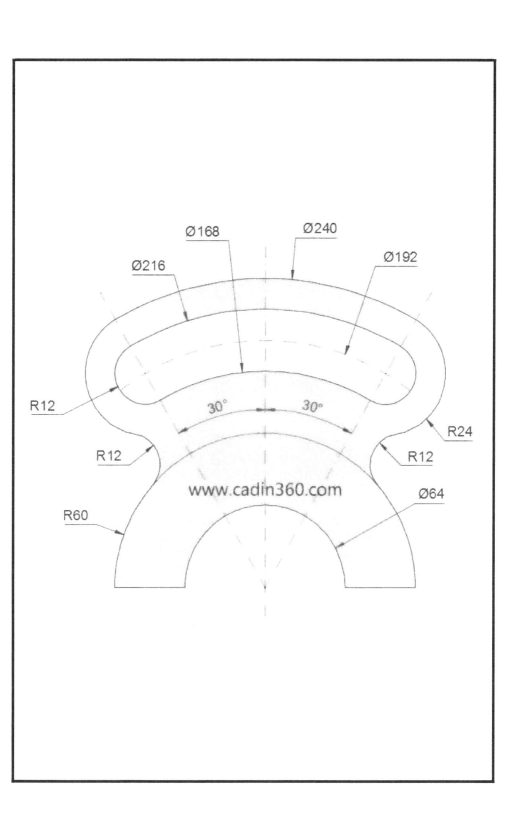

Ø168 Ø240 Ø192 Ø216 R12 R12 R24 R12 R60 Ø64 30° 30° www.cadin360.com

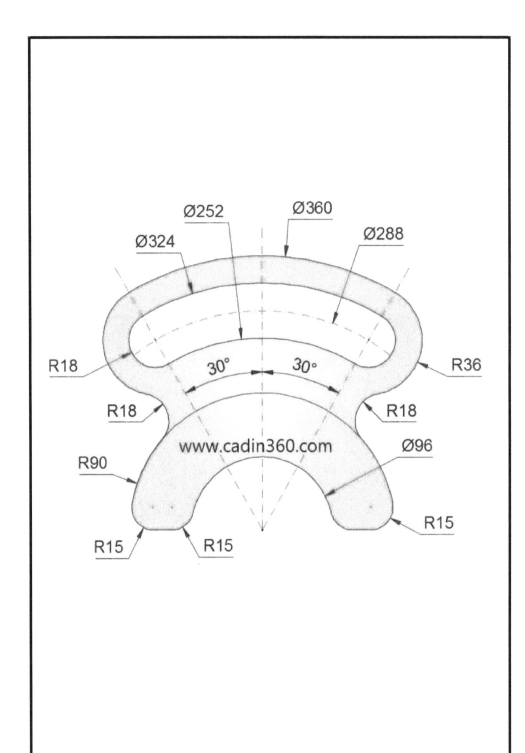

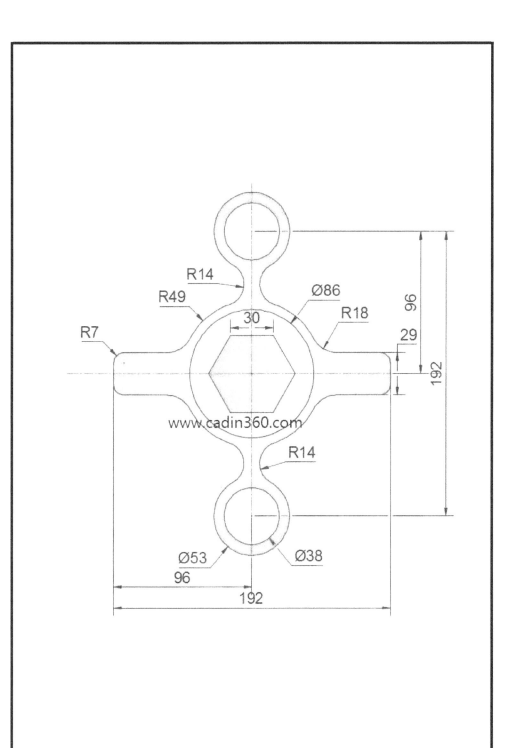

R14

R49

Ø86

R18

R7

30

96

29

192

www.cadin360.com

R14

Ø53

Ø38

96

192

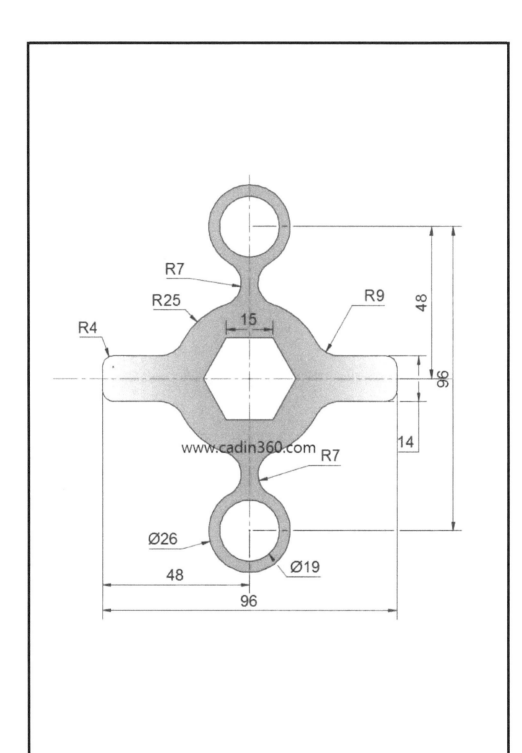

R7

R25

R9

R4

15

48

96

14

www.cadin360.com R7

Ø26

Ø19

48

96

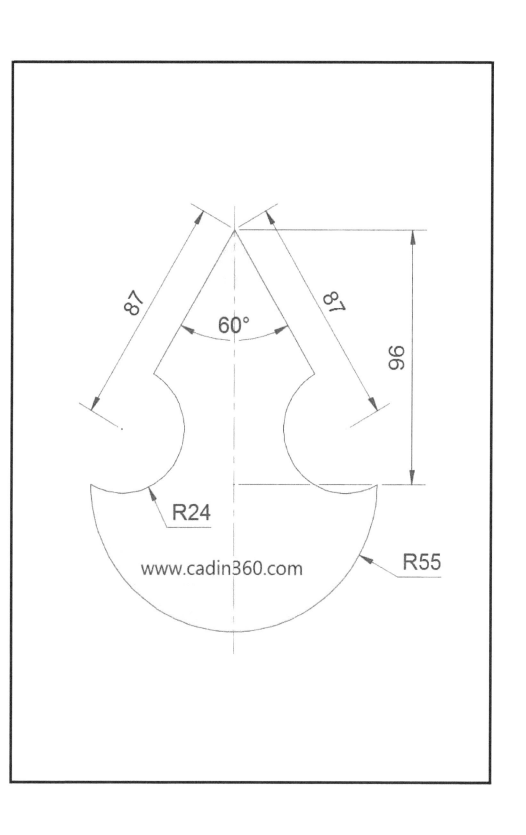

87

87

60°

96

R24

www.cadin360.com

R55

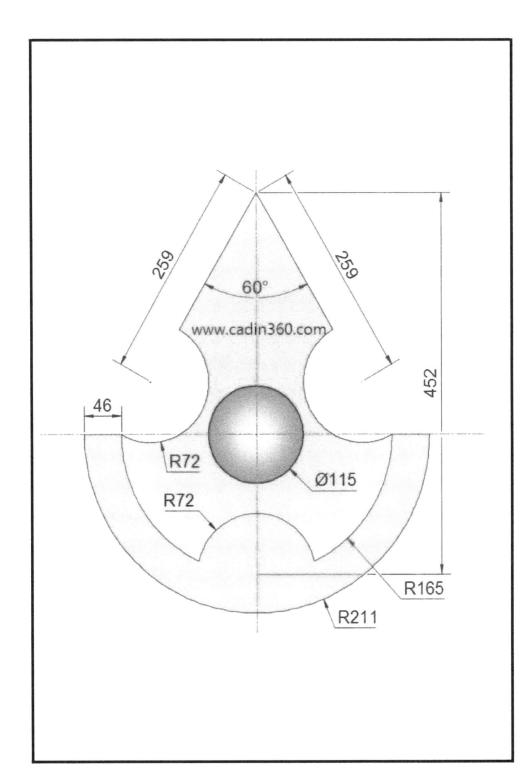

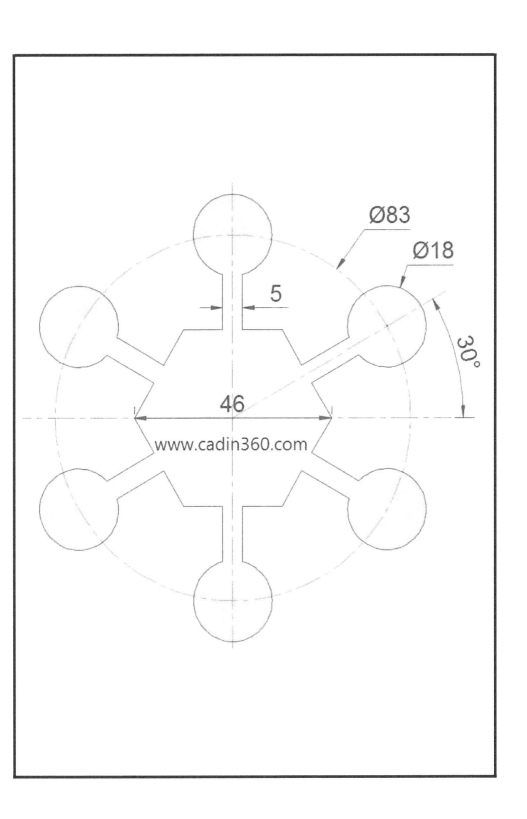

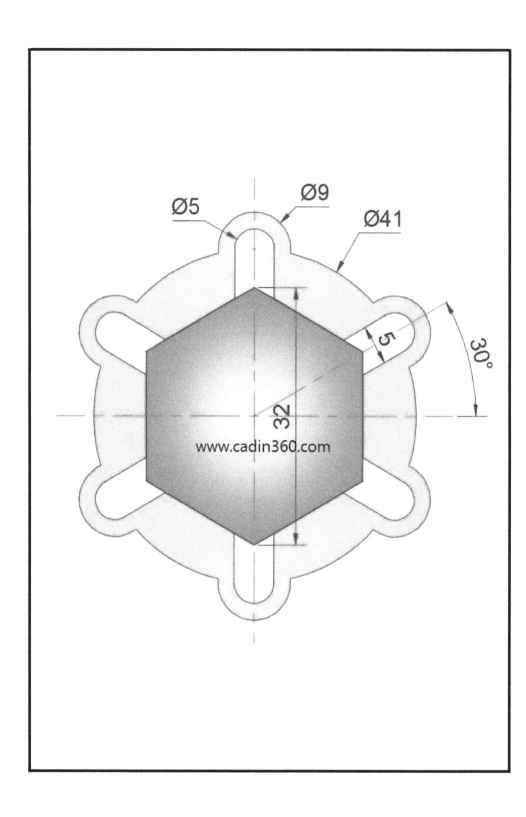

Ø5

Ø9

Ø41

5

30°

32

www.cadin360.com

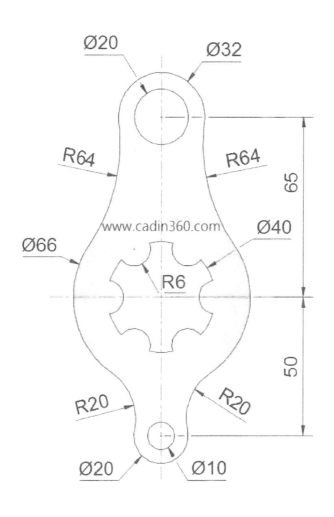

Ø20   Ø32

R64   R64

65

www.cadin360.com   Ø40

Ø66   R6

50

R20   R20

Ø20   Ø10

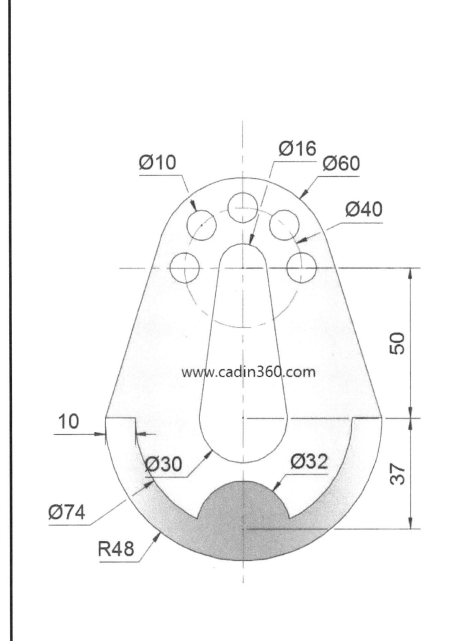

Ø10 Ø16 Ø60 Ø40

50

10

Ø30 Ø32

37

Ø74

R48

www.cadin360.com

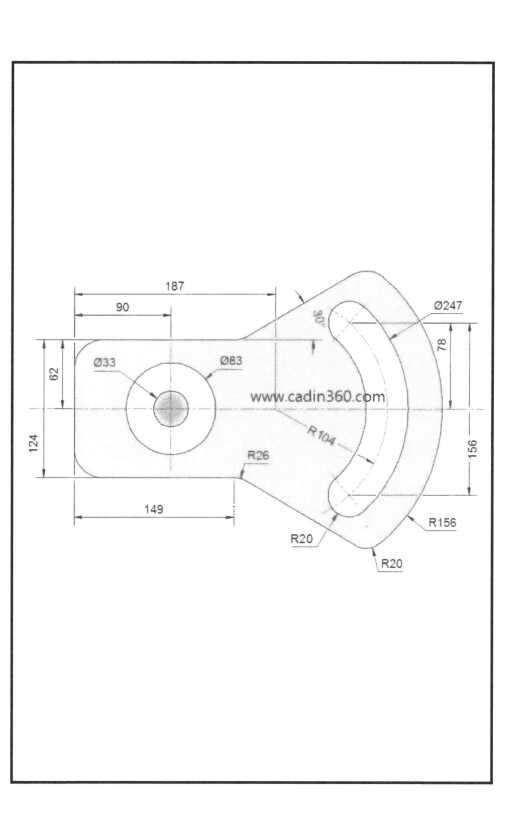

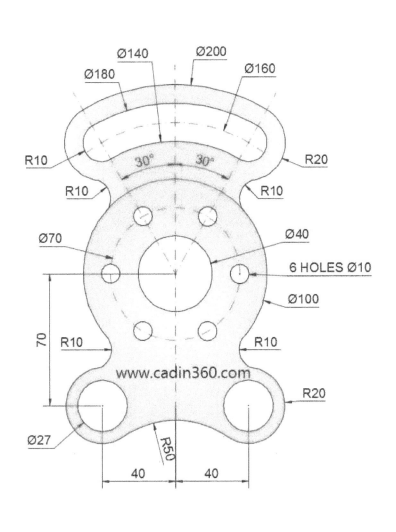

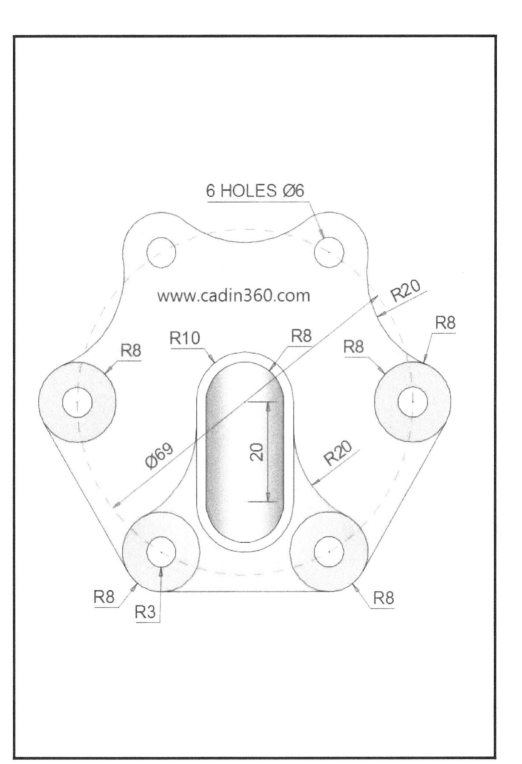

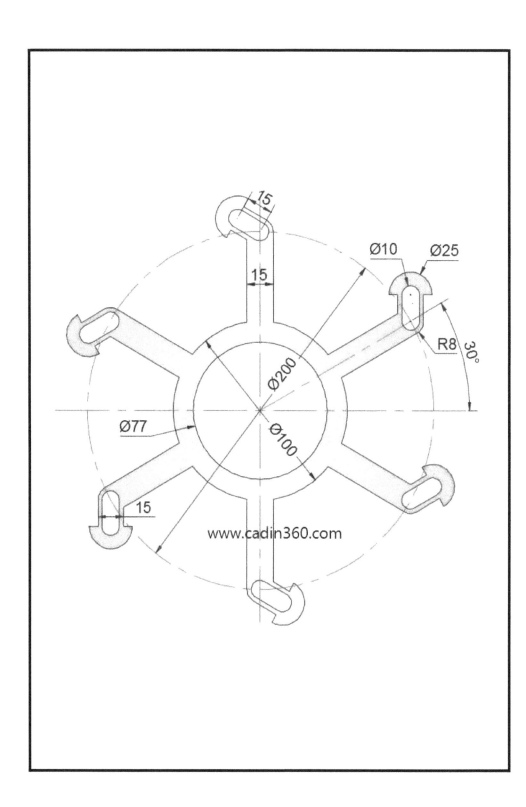

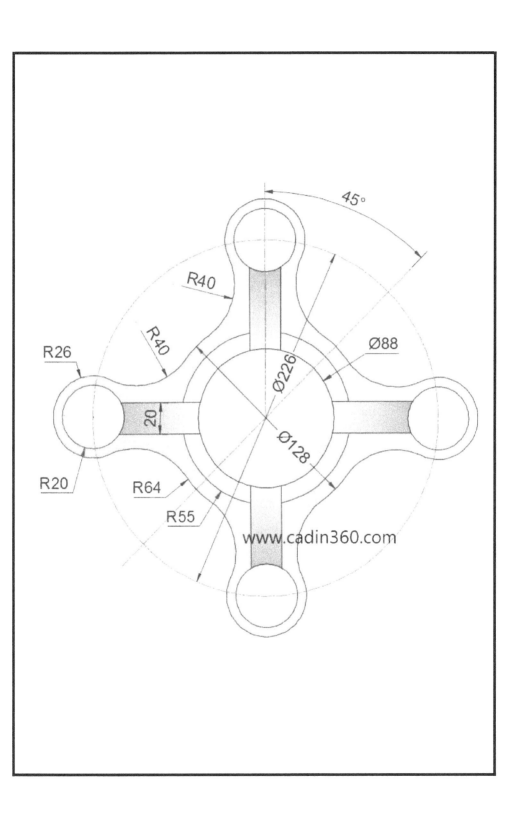

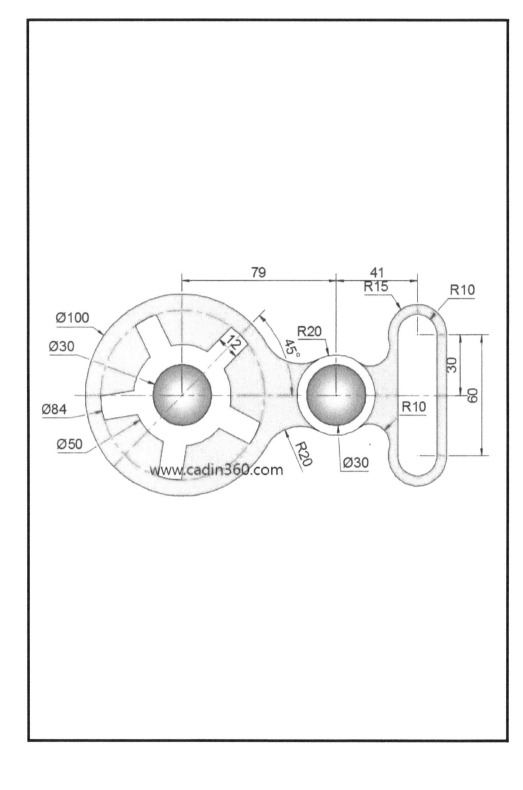

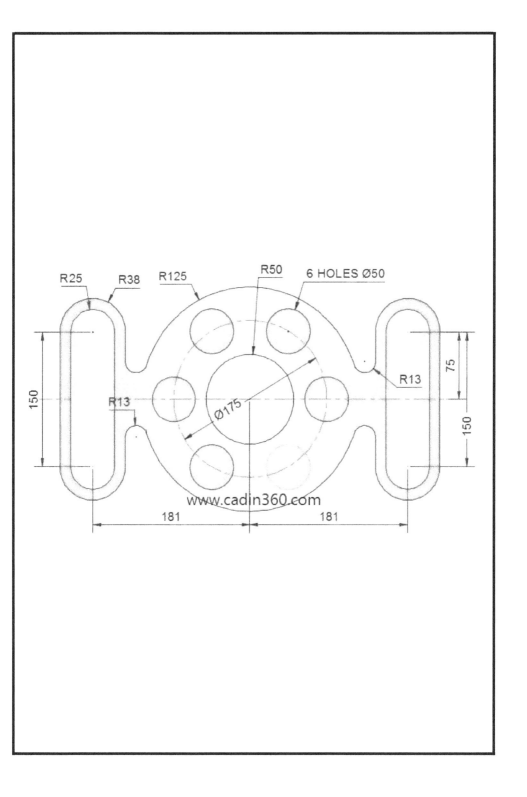

R25 R38 R125 R50 6 HOLES Ø50

R13

150

R13

Ø175

75

150

181 181

www.cadin360.com

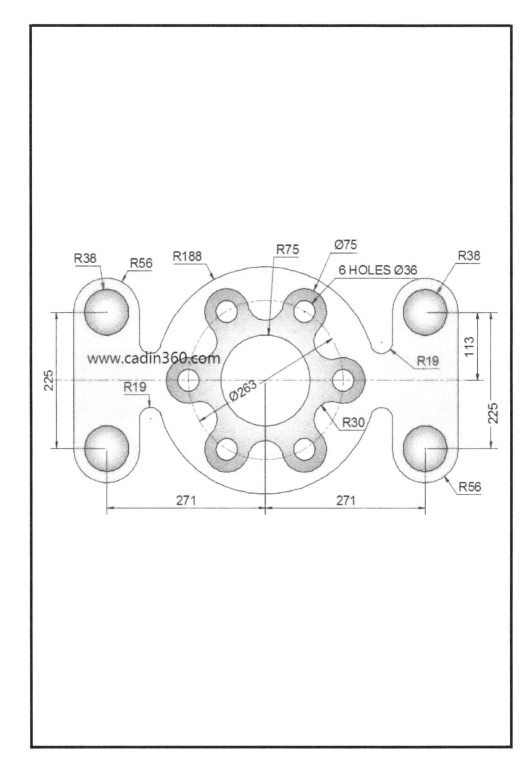

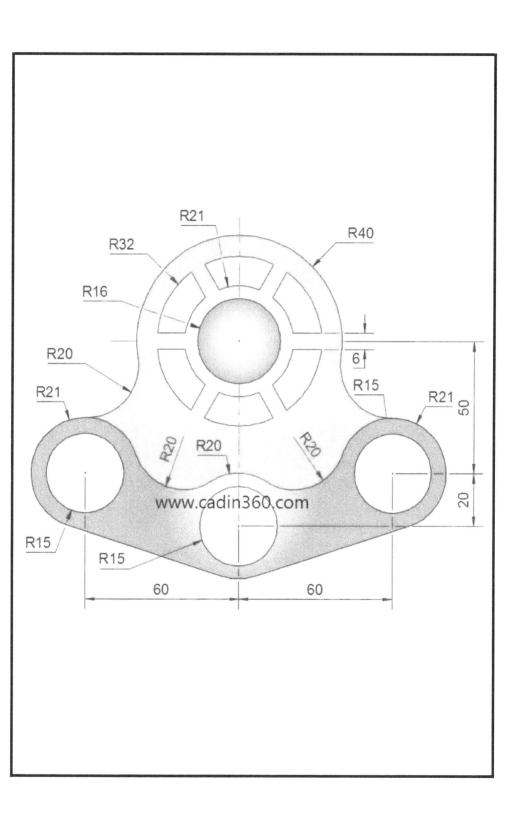

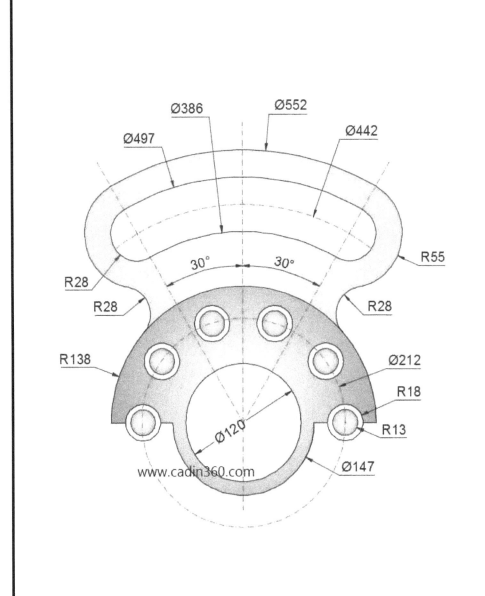

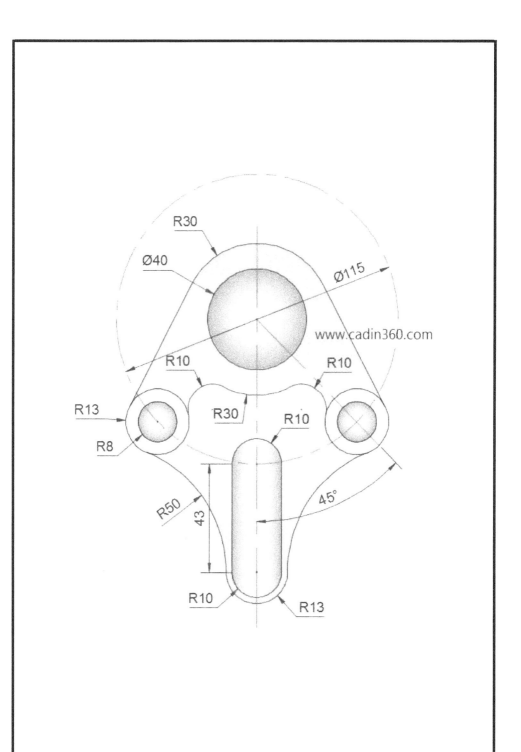
www.cadin360.com

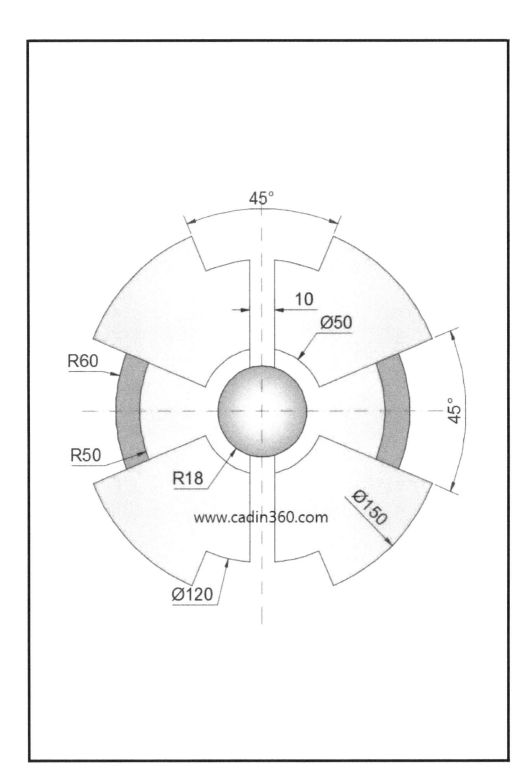

45°

10

Ø50

R60

R50

R18

www.cadin360.com

45°

Ø150

Ø120

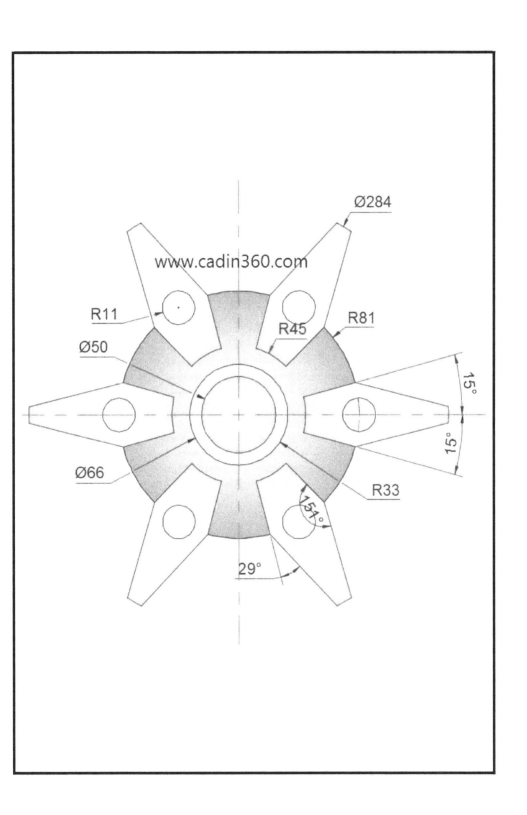

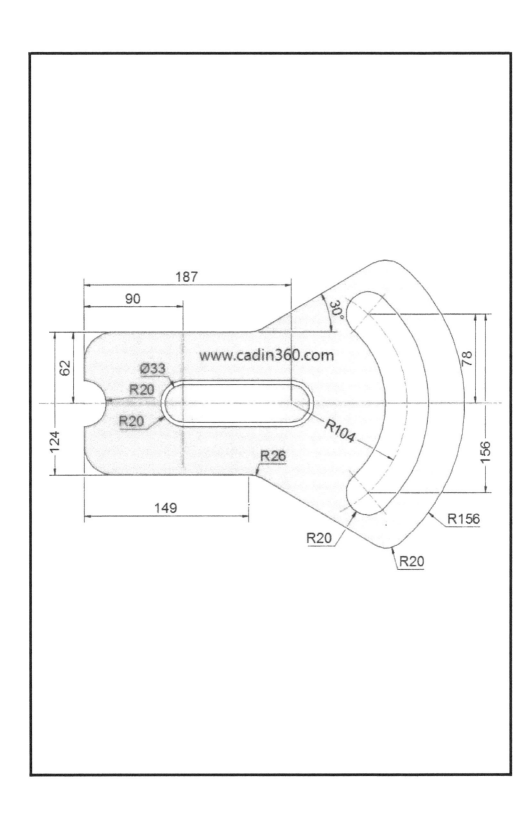

www.cadin360.com

3D EXERCISES

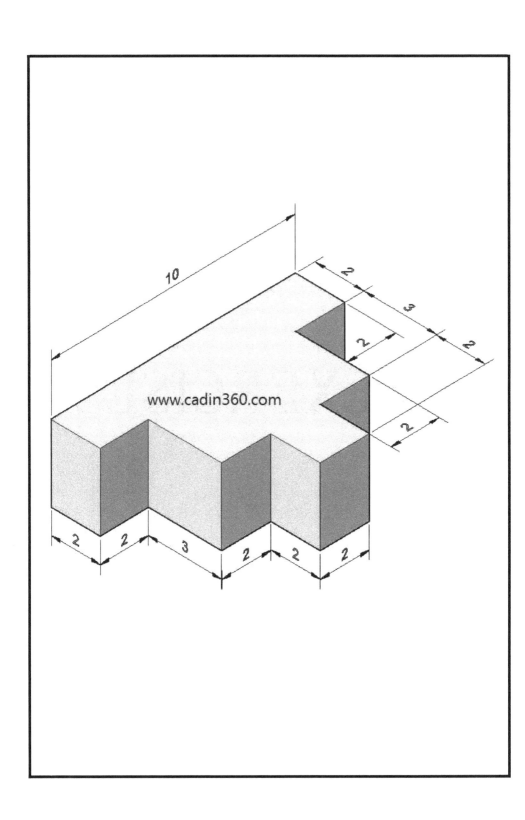

www.cadin360.com

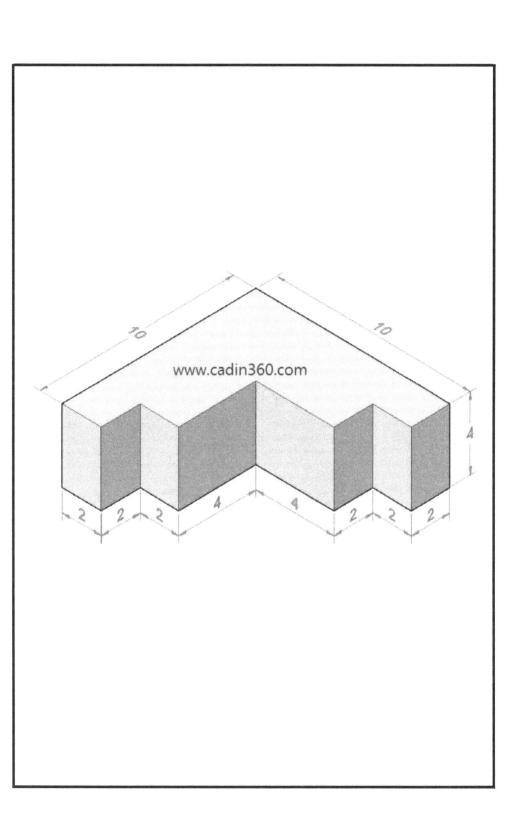
www.cadin360.com

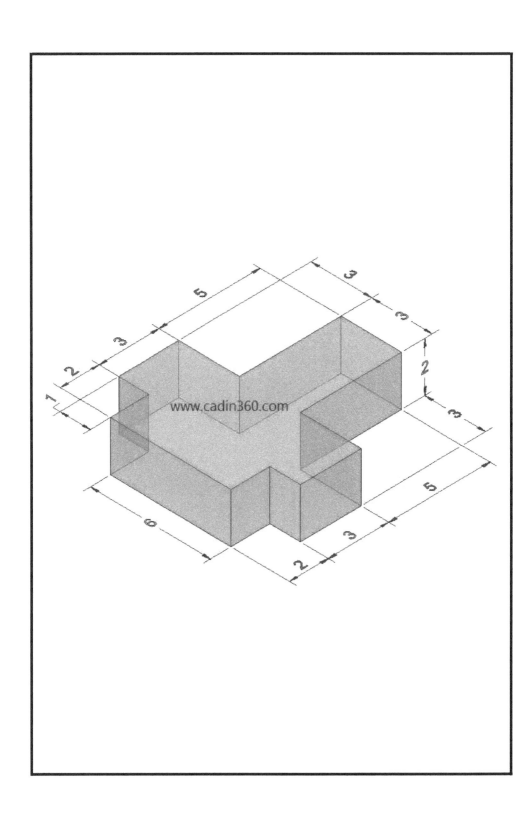

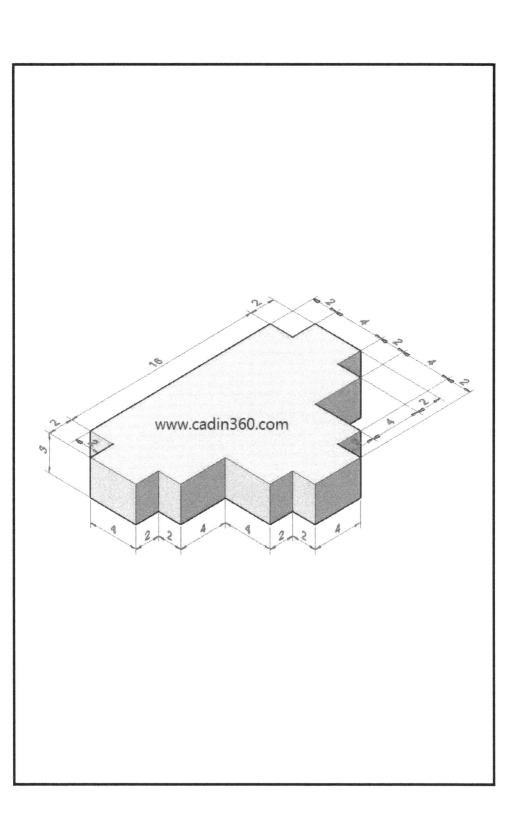

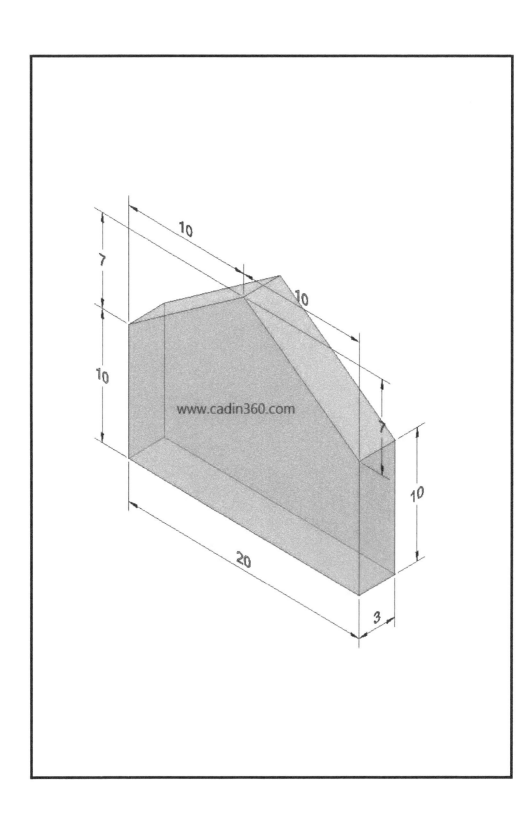

10

7

10

10

10

7

20

10

3

www.cadin360.com

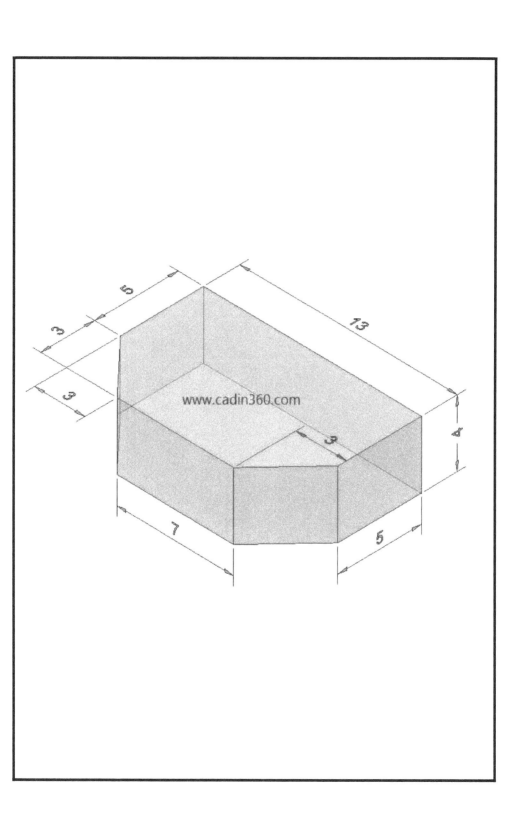

5

3

3

13

3

www.cadin360.com

4

7

5

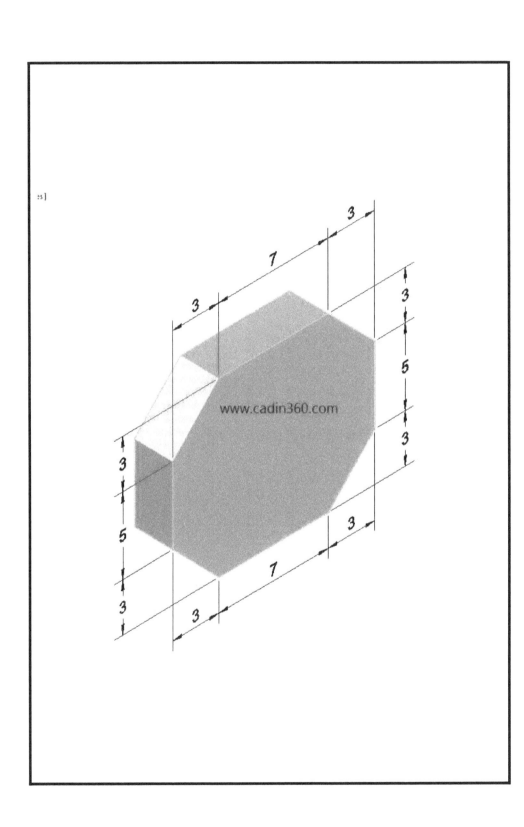

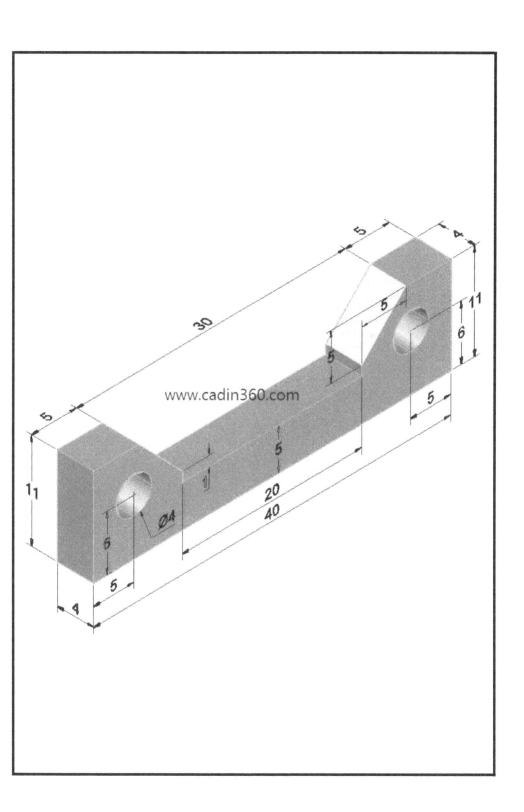

www.cadin360.com

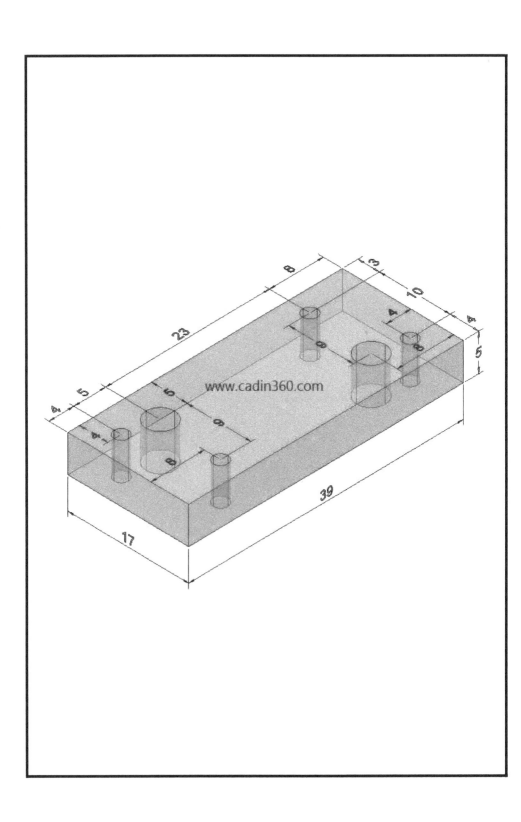

www.cadin360.com

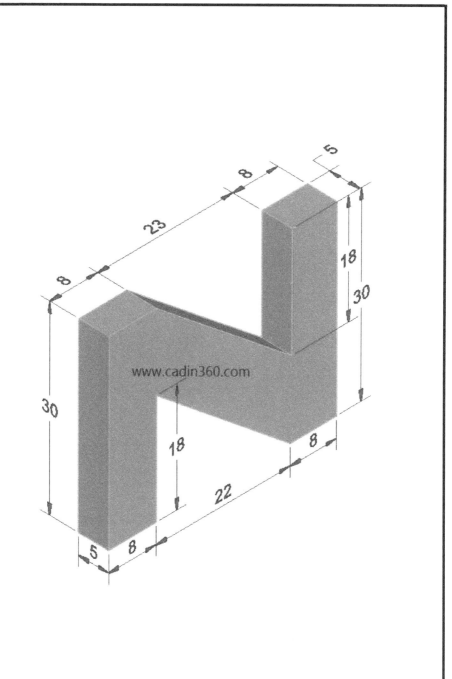

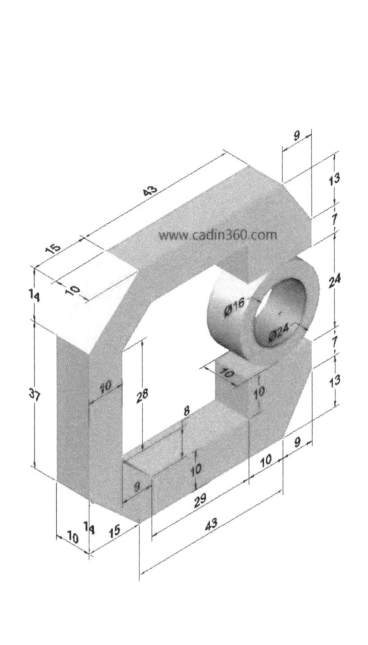
www.cadin360.com

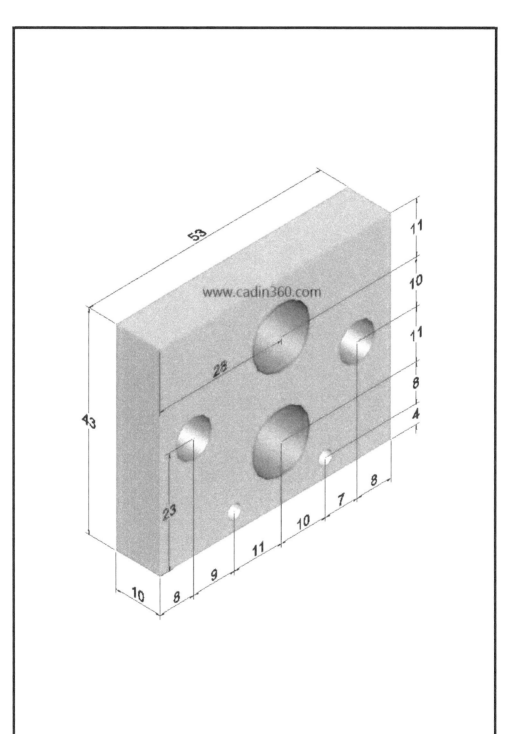
www.cadin360.com

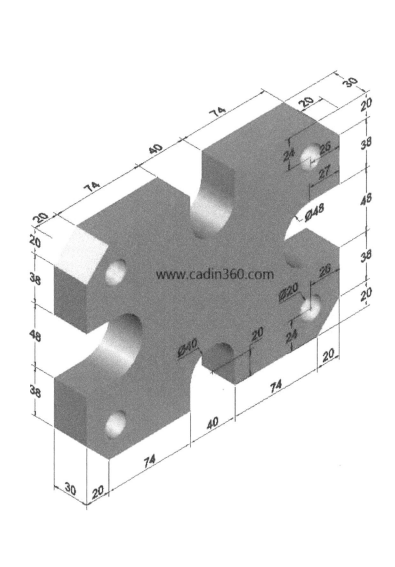

www.cadin360.com

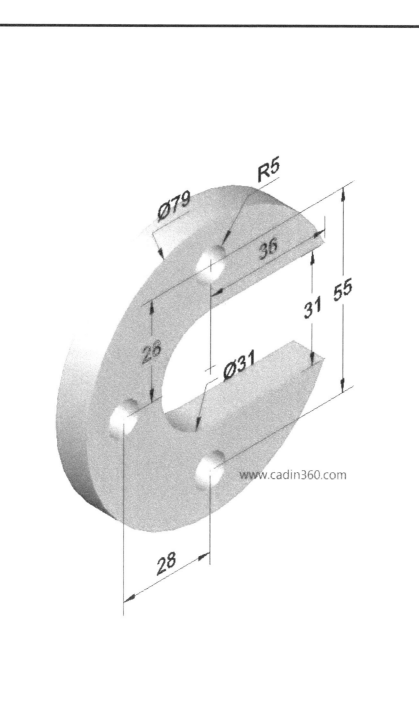

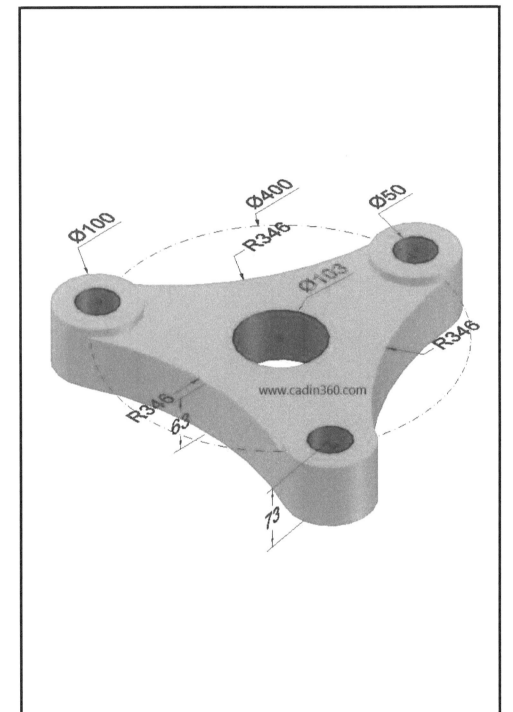

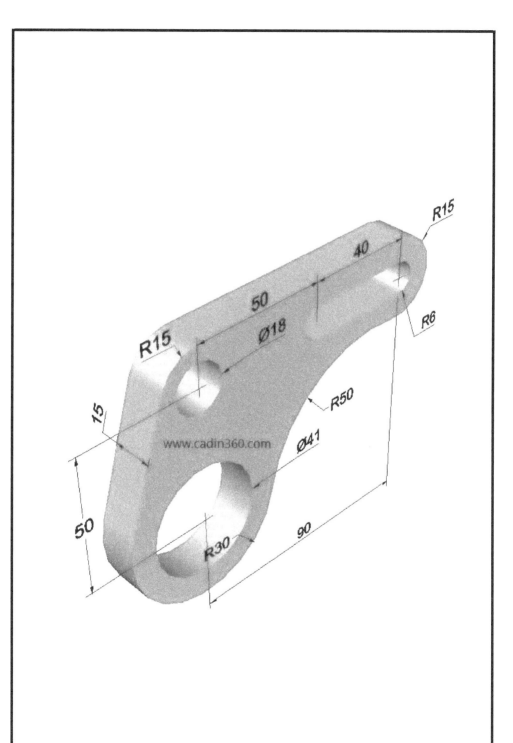

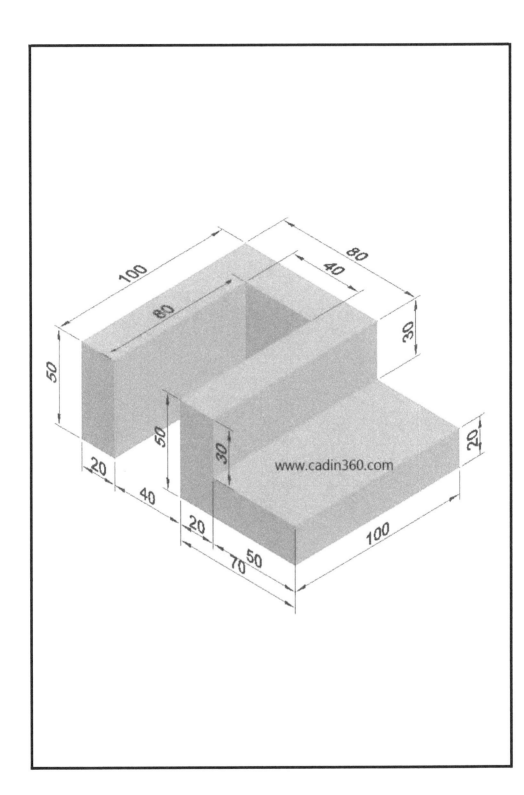

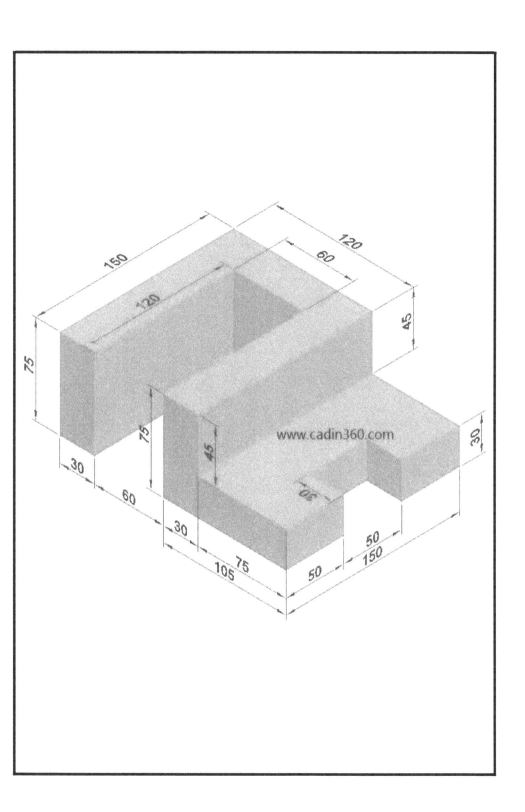

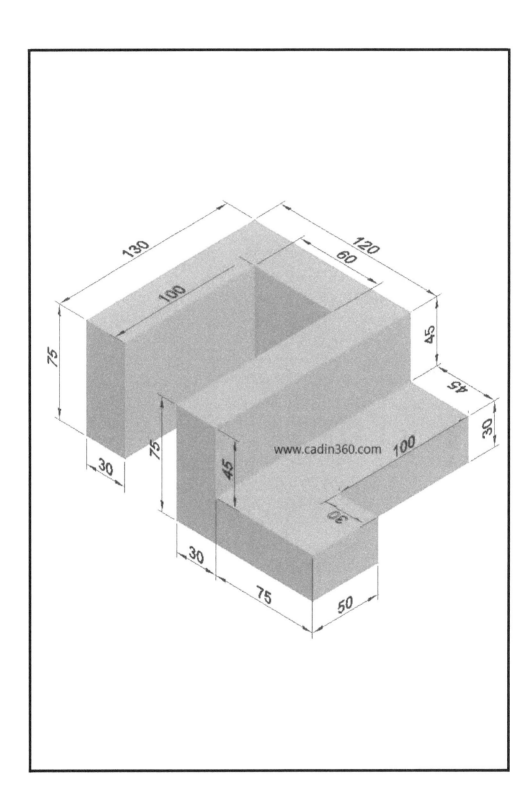

www.cadin360.com

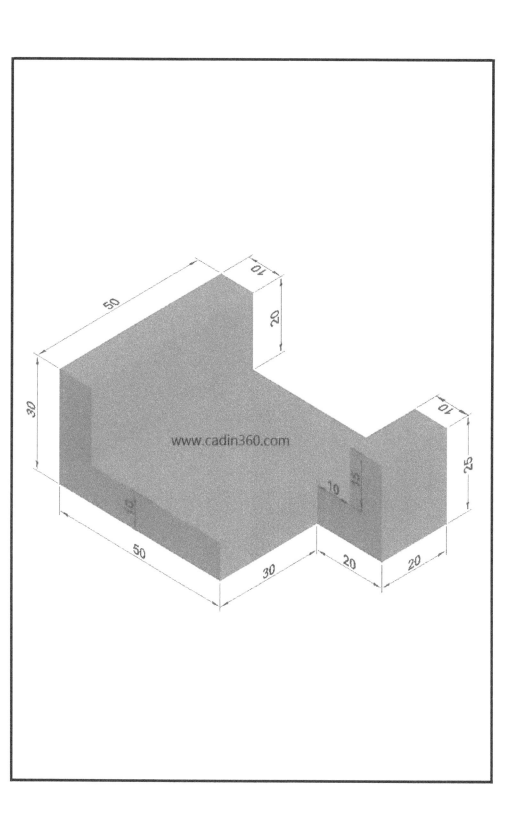

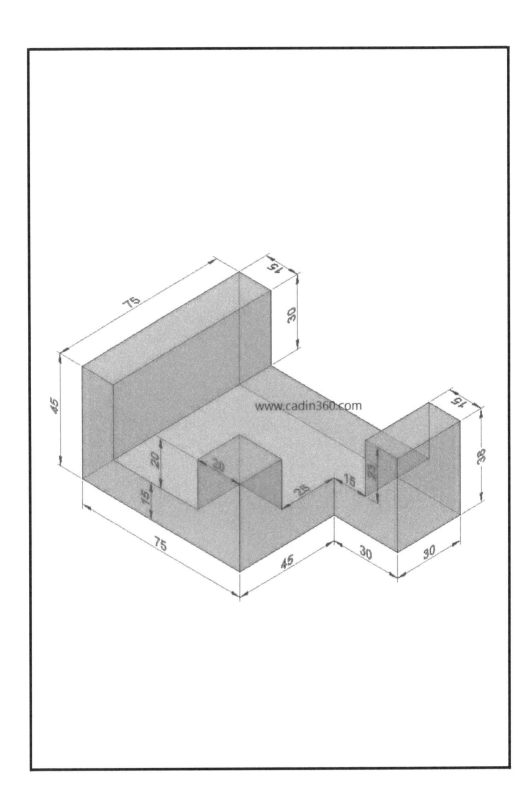

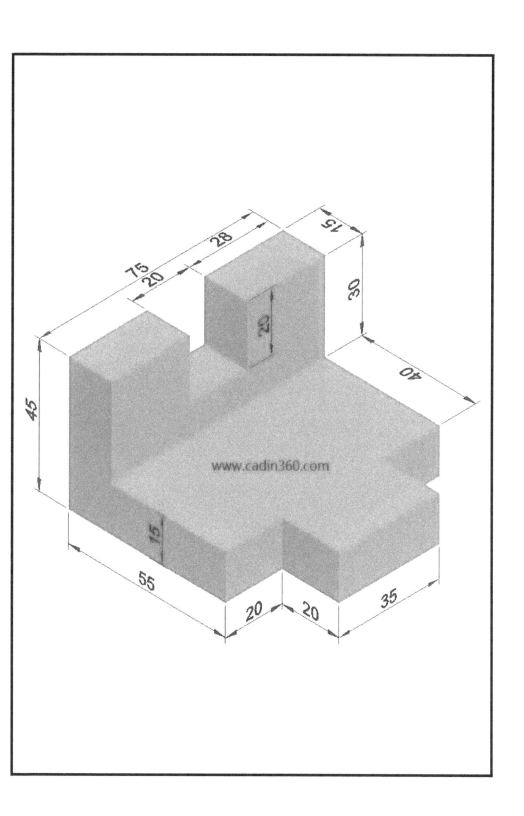

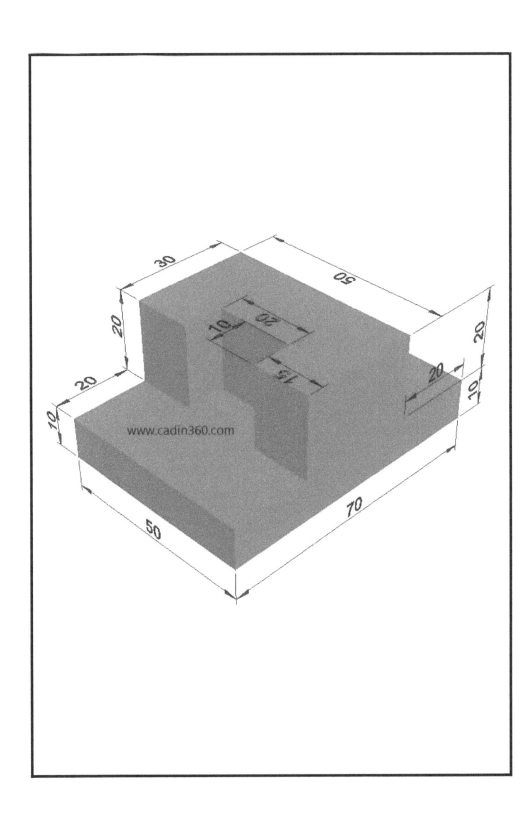
www.cadin360.com

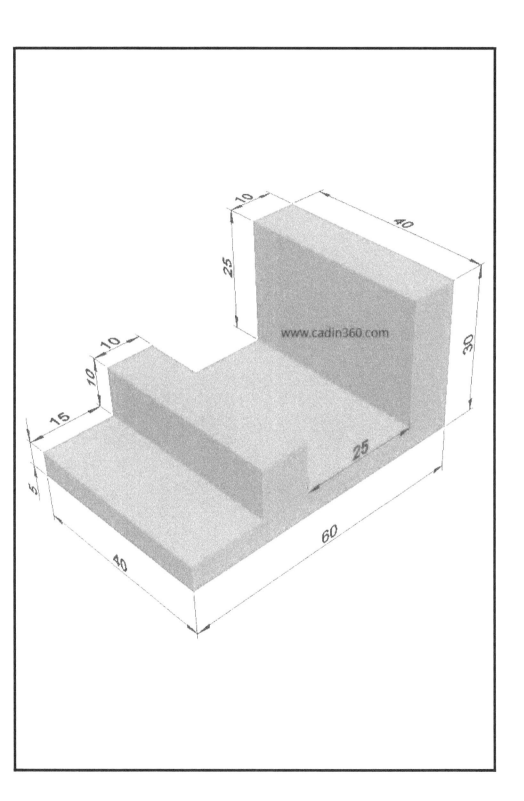

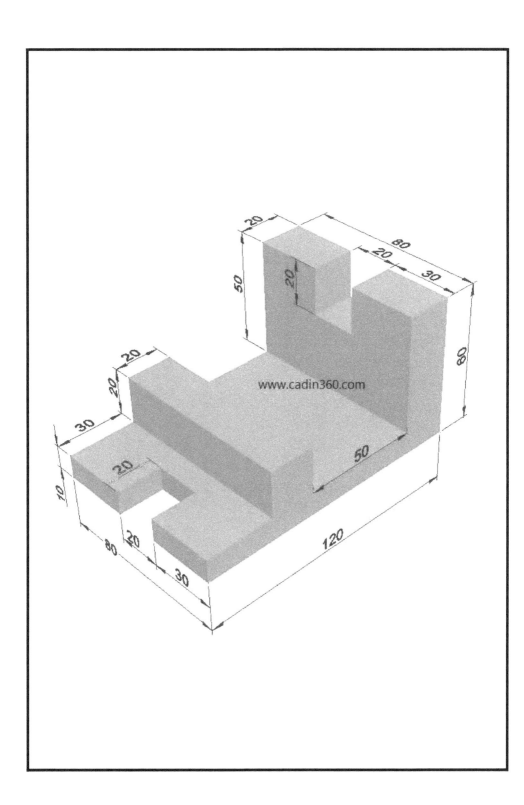

www.cadin360.com

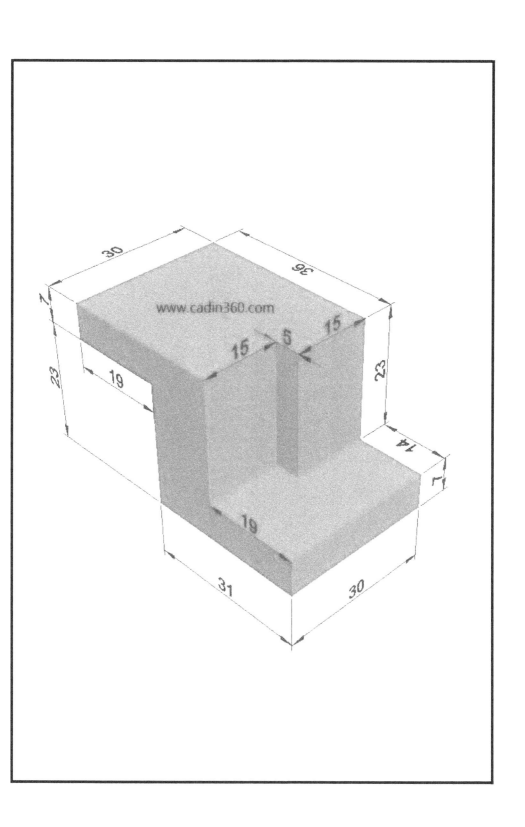

www.cadin360.com

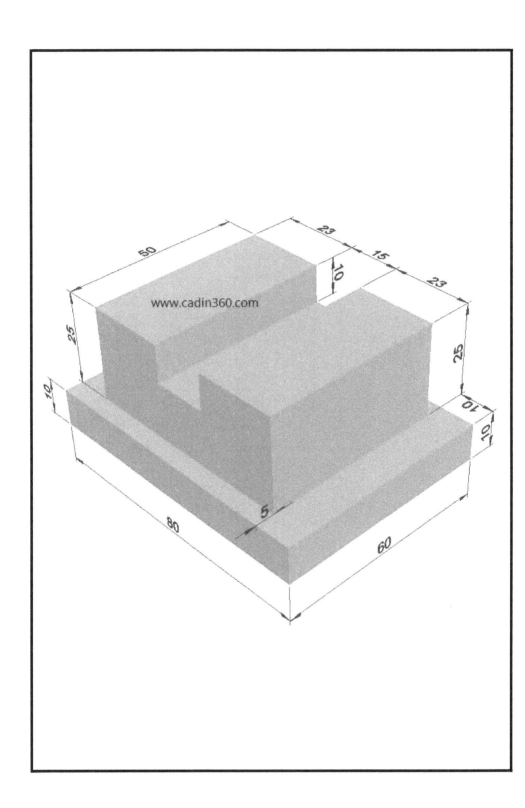

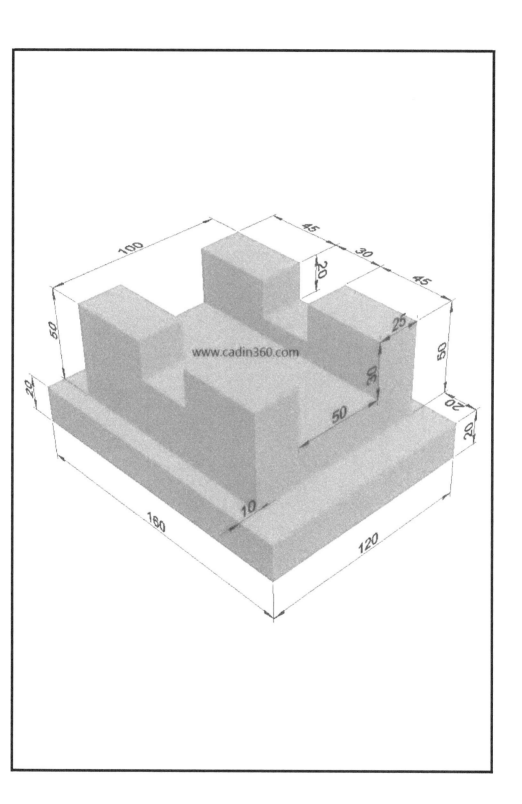

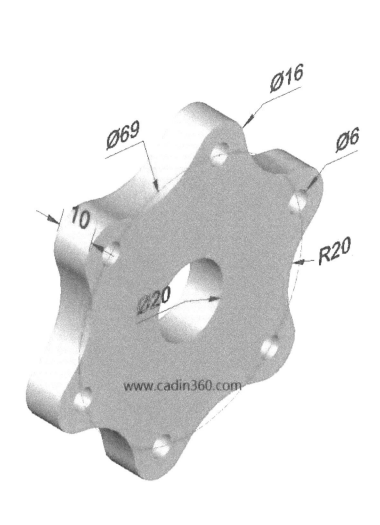

Ø16

Ø69

Ø6

10

R20

Ø20

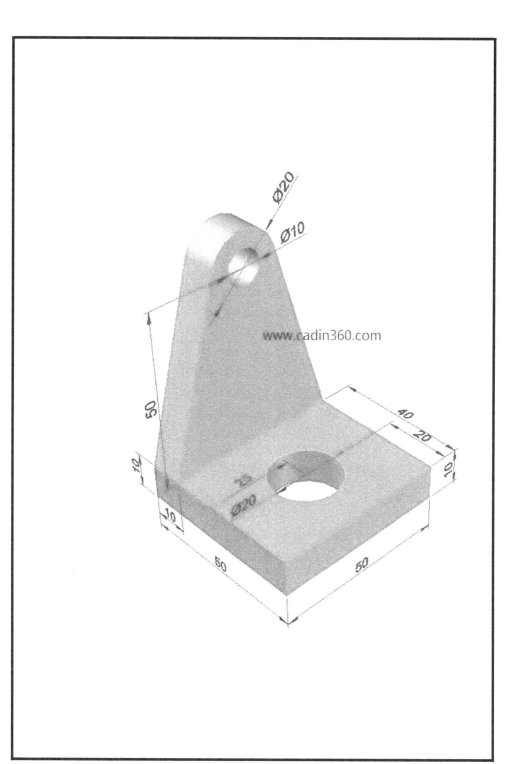

www.cadin360.com

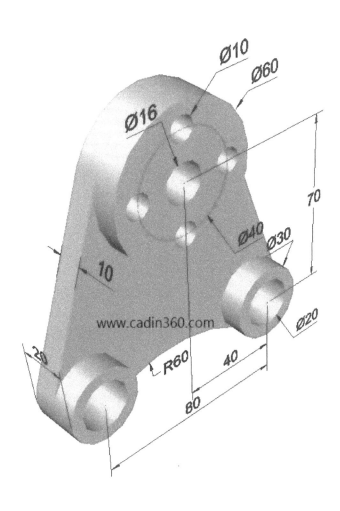

Ø10
Ø60
Ø16
70
10
Ø40
Ø30
www.cadin360.com
Ø20
20
R60
40
80

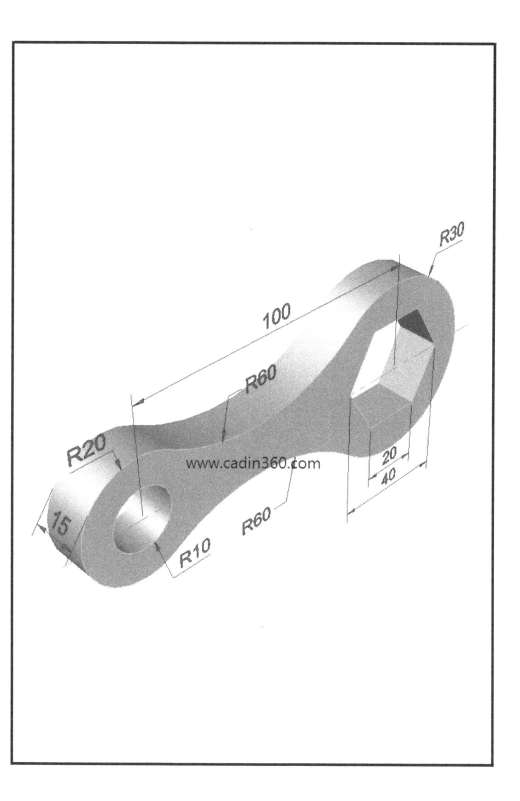

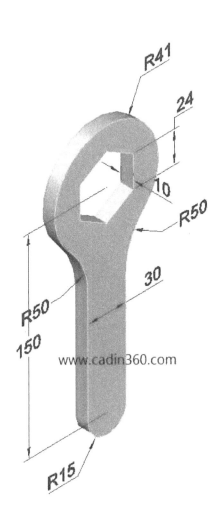

R41

24

10

R50

30

R50

150

R15

www.cadin360.com

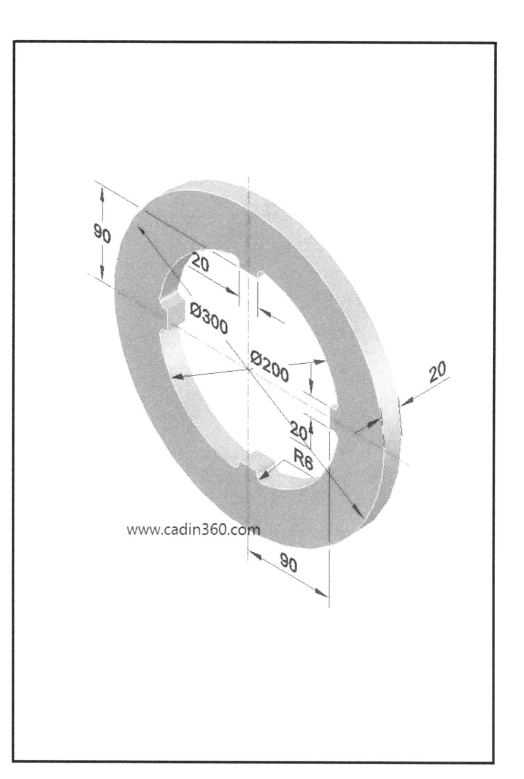

90

20

Ø300

Ø200

20

20

R6

www.cadin360.com

90

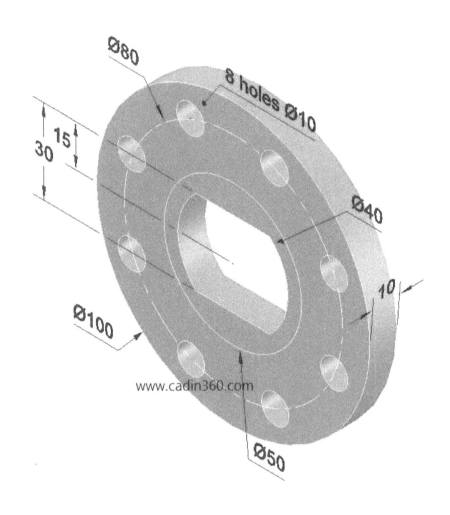

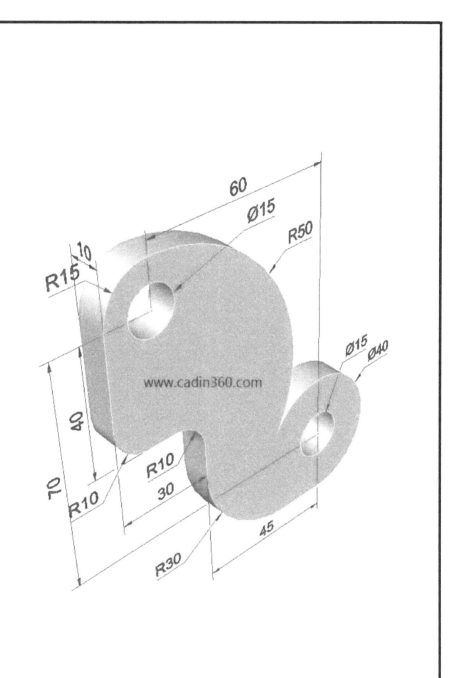

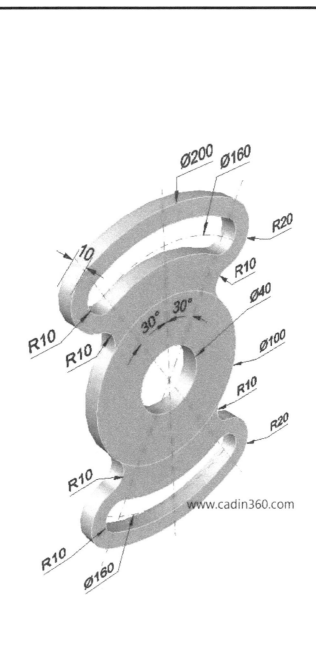

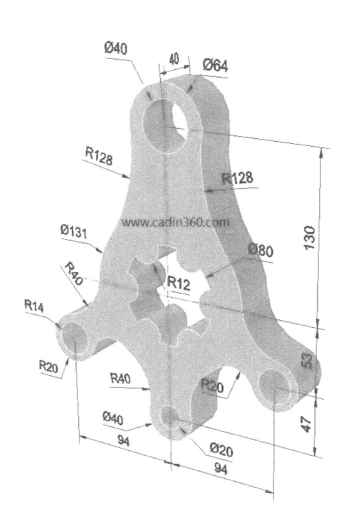

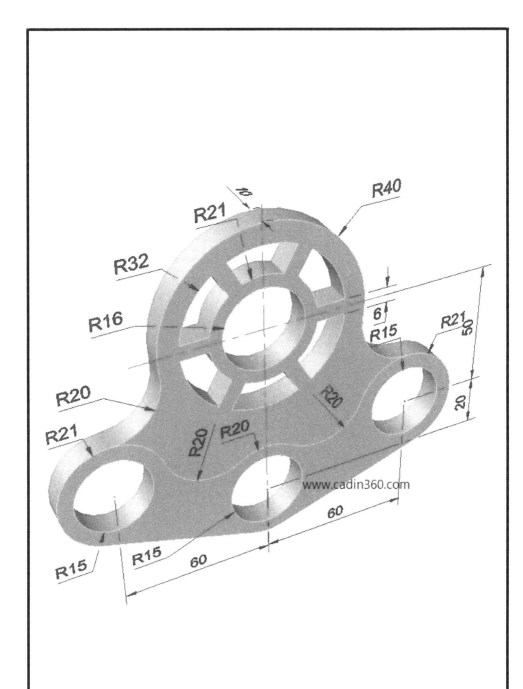

R21
R40
R32
R16
R20
R21
R15
R20
R20
R20
R15
R15
60
60
6
50
20
www.cadin360.com

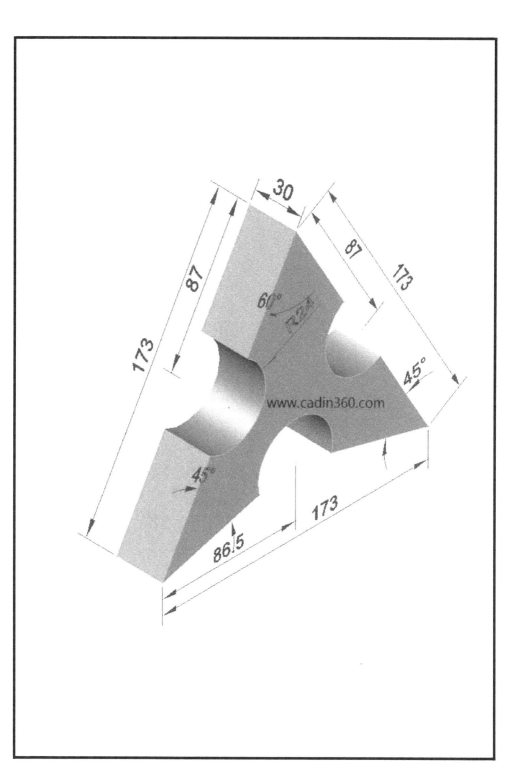

www.cadin360.com

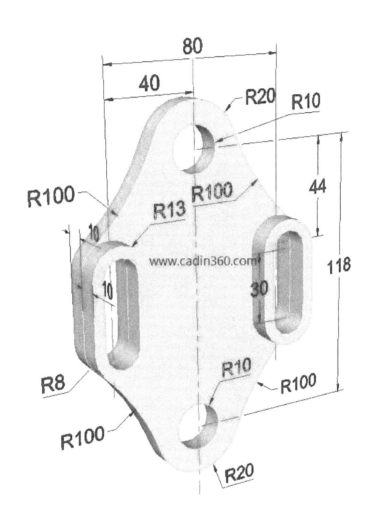

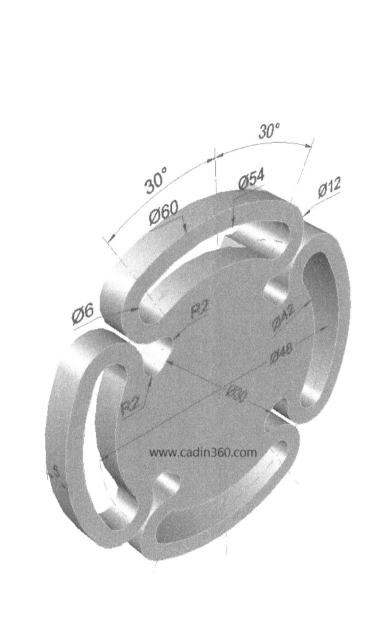

www.cadin360.com

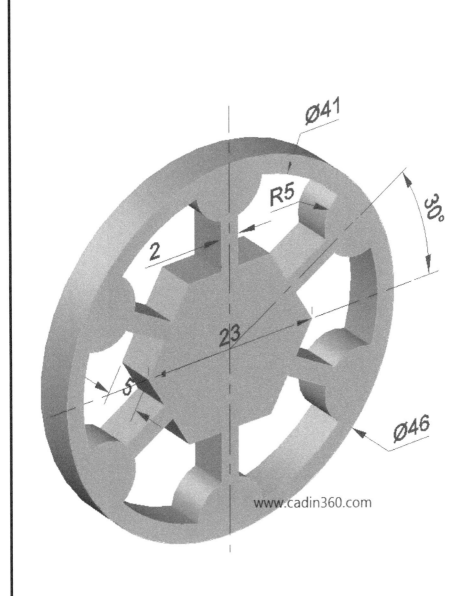

Ø41

R5

30°

2

23

5

Ø46

www.cadin360.com

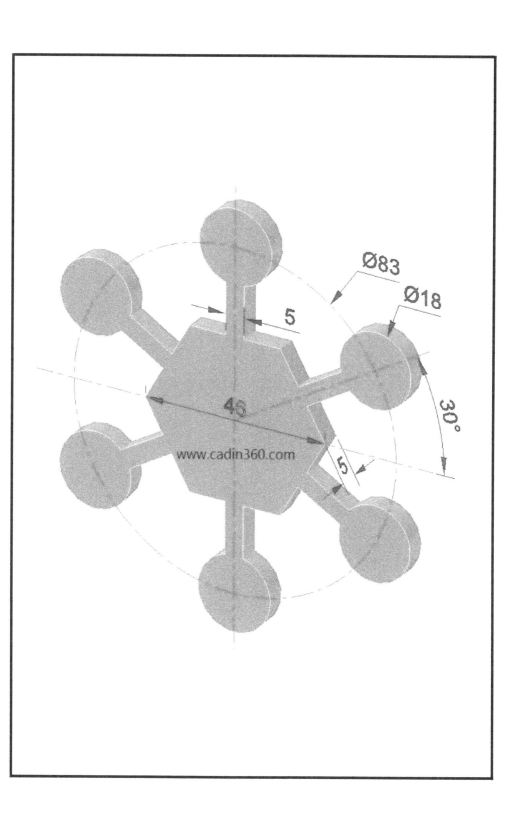

Ø83

Ø18

5

46

30°

5

www.cadin360.com

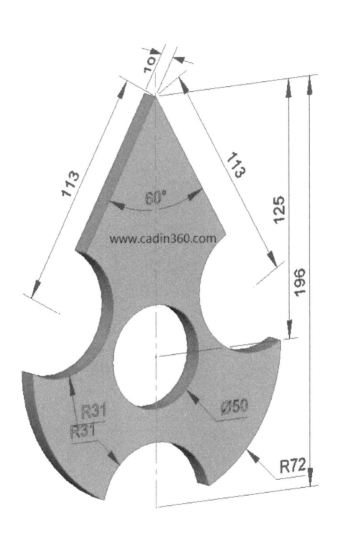

www.cadin360.com

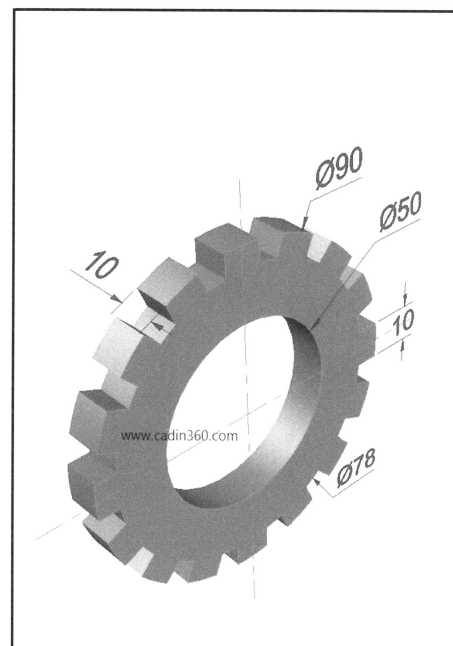

Ø90

Ø50

10

10

Ø78

www.cadin360.com

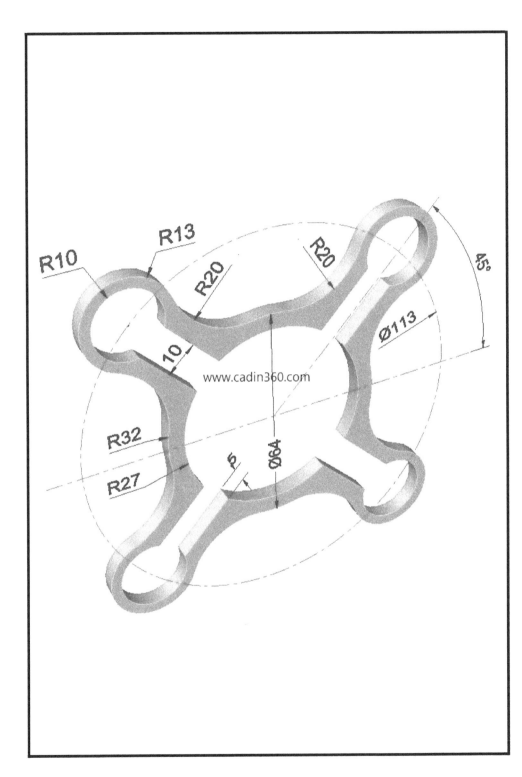

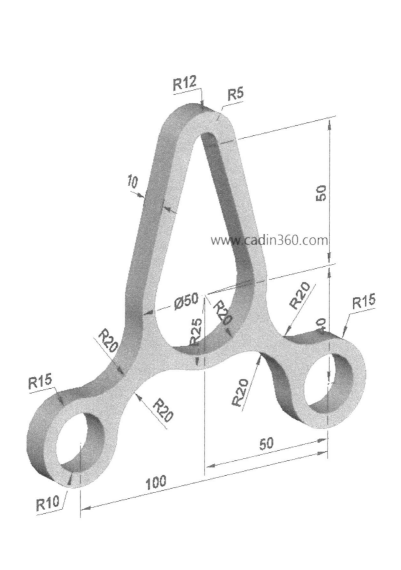

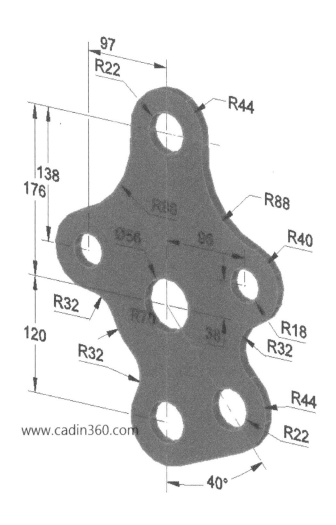

www.cadin360.com

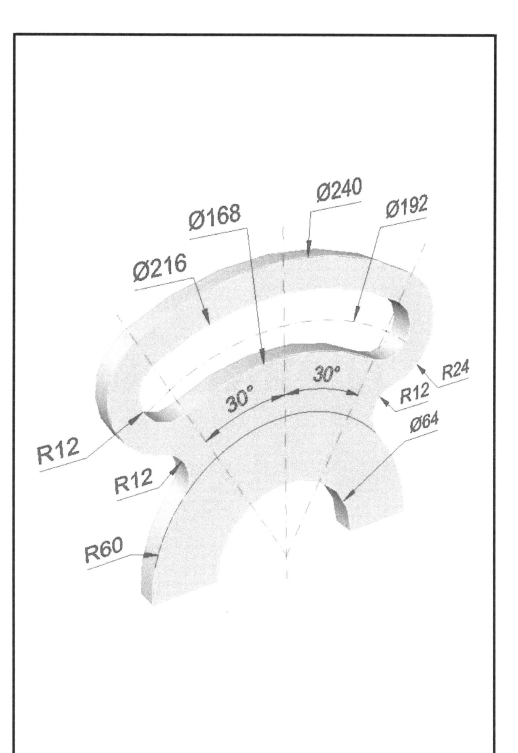

Thank You